Motorbooks International Illustrated Buy

Illustrated

Lincoln

BUYER'S ★ GUIDE™

Paul R. Woudenberg

Motorbooks International
Publishers & Wholesalers ®

First published in 1990 by Motorbooks International Publishers & Wholesalers, P O Box 2, 729 Prospect Avenue, Osceola, WI 54020 USA

Motorbooks International books are also available at discounts in bulk quantity for industrial or sales-promotional use. For details write to Special Sales Manager at the Publisher's address

Library of Congress Cataloging-in-Publication Data
Woudenberg, Paul R.
　　Illustrated Lincoln buyer's guide / Paul R. Woudenberg.
　　　　p.　cm. — (Motorbooks International illustrated buyer's guide series)
　　Includes bibliographical references.
　　ISBN 0-87938-430-1
　　1. Lincoln automobile—Purchasing.　2. Lincoln automobile—Collectors and collecting.　I. Title. II. Series.
　　TL215.L5W67　1990　　　　　90-31888
　　629.222′2—dc20　　　　　　　CIP

On the front cover: This 1964 Lincoln Continental convertible is owned by David Wald. *Village Photography*
On the back cover: This 1970 "Dual Cowl Phaeton" Mark III show car was displayed at the 1970 Chicago Auto Show. *Ford Motor Company* A 1946 Lincoln Continental cabriolet owned by Walter Williamson. *Tim Howley*

Printed and bound in the United States of America

Contents

Acknowledgments

The Lincoln & Continental Owners Club has been most helpful in the research of this book. Numerous members have written me with suggestions and pictures. Others have been generous with their time in answering phone questions. The author wishes to thank the officers of the club for their cooperation and encouragement.

In particular, Tim Howley, the able editor of *Continental Comments*, has shared his Lincoln editorial experience along with photographs from his extensive archives. He has read the manuscript and has given many helpful suggestions. Bob Kellner, long time member of the club, has been most encouraging and has also read the manuscript. His observations and suggestions have been a marvelous help.

Readers are not responsible for errors. Although the author has made every effort to produce an error free book, perfection is not granted in this life. Corrections, criticisms, and opinions are most welcome.

Personnel of the Ford Motor Company have made available their resources. Cheryl M. Crawford of the Corporate News Department has been very helpful along with Mr. Ordowski of the Photographic Library. Don Petersen, retired CEO of the Ford Motor Company, provided his usual gracious help in expediting all matters.

Editor Greg Field of Motorbooks has wisely shepherded this book through the various stages and the author is grateful for his help.

Owners have been identified in picture captions wherever possible. Cars may have been sold since these pictures were captioned. The author would be delighted to hear from new owners and make appropriate corrections in forthcoming printings. Likewise, information on unidentified cars will be appreciated.

The author has carefully reviewed *Continental Comments* in search of owner experience with particular regard to problems. He is indebted to the many enthusiasts who have shared their wisdom with club members in this splendid magazine. Below is a list of the individuals whose observations have been used and the author wishes to thank them all for their help.

Chapter 1: Steve Hastings, H. H. Nutting, Lloyd E. Pearson, Seymour Petrovsky, Dave Cole, S. H. Barrington and Jim Baker
Chapter 2: Bob Petrucelli, Dr. John L. Mansell and OCee Ritch
Chapter 4: Gary Schwertley
Chapter 5: Gary Schwertley and Bob Davis
Chapter 6: Robert J. Prins, John LeBaron, Bob Davis, James Donaven, Bill Coughlin and Marvin Arnold
Chapter 7: Grady Jacoway and Bob French
Chapter 8: Wes Joplin, Tim Howley, Ron Baker and Hank Pittman
Chapter 10: Marvin Arnold and Lewis B. Scott

Preface
Why Buy a Lincoln?

1. The Lincoln has always been a great car. From its noble beginnings in the hands of Henry M. Leland to the most recent offerings, the Lincoln has stood for quality without compromise. The Mark II was built to an unprecedented industry standard, while the 1961 Continental broke new ground in assembly precision.

2. Mechanical innovation has been a hallmark of the Lincoln. The unit body construction used in the early Zephyrs, and repeated in 1958 and afterwards, was imaginative and daring. The much-maligned V–12 engine, used from 1936 to 1948, has turned out to be far better than most would have guessed. The great performance engines of the early fifties dominated the Mexican Road Races. The Mark VII introduced suspension and roadholding competence heretofore reserved for only the most exotic cars.

3. The Lincoln has always been a styling innovator. Edsel Ford's leadership ensured that the L and K models were equal to anything in the "classic" trade. The Zephyr was, in 1936, a wildly novel car that "worked" commercially, while Edsel's Continental was regarded with awe from the moment it first appeared, a love which has never faded. John Reinhart's Mark II was a standout of controlled elegance in a time of outrageous styling flamboyance. The Continental of 1961 was a stunning car and built Lincoln's fortunes to unprecedented heights. The Mark III was another styling triumph. Who can

doubt that the recent products of Lincoln have once again captured styling leadership?

4. The Lincoln has strong club support. The Lincoln & Continental Owner's Club (L.C.O.C.) was founded in 1953, one of the first clubs for American-made cars. The Lincoln-Zephyr Club, founded in 1968, has cooperated in numerous ventures for the general good of the marque. Buyers of Lincolns can join the Lincoln & Continental Owner's Club with the expectation of discovering a circle of friends eager to help with restoration and technical matters. The club chapters offer numerous rallies, concours and activities which bring together Lincoln enthusiasts for fun and happy motoring. The club also produces a fine magazine, *Continental Comments*, filled with club information, technical material, historical and interesting sidelights which knits the club together, as well as a cross-referencing directory which allows members to seek out one another for neighborly support.

5. The Lincoln, in almost every model form, has been rapidly appreciating in price. This has encouraged restoration and has rewarded long-time owners for their faith and perseverance.

6. The Lincoln is one of those very rare cars whose collecting support has carried over into recent production. Ten years ago, few would have guessed that the Mark IV and Mark V would become collectibles, complete with fresh literature, rising prices and

concours judging classes. That lesson has not been lost on current buyers who have come to view *all* Lincolns as potential collectibles. There is no other American car that has found this favor, and it is a remarkable testimony to the power of the marque. Even the Mark VII and the Town Car are viewed with an unusual contemporary enthusiasm which leads straight to collectibility.

7. The Lincoln is a great driving car. The reputation as the premiere cross-country touring car, established by the Model L of the twenties, has not faded. The early Lincolns were tough and reliable. The Lincoln-Zephyr was a revelation of smoothness to buyers in the late-thirties. The flathead V-8s of 1949 were strong cars able to manage sustained high speeds without problems. Few will deny that the great 1952–54 V-8s were the finest road cars in America and the later Mark Series were also highway favorites. Recent production has once again emphasized that Lincoln remains a driver's car.

8. The Lincoln-Mercury Division remains supportive of collectors and enthusiasts. The personalities who guided the fortunes of the country are accessible, and their enthusiasm for the cars goes beyond corporate responsibility. There is the feeling that Lincoln executives really *like* cars. The support of the company is evident at the numerous national Lincoln meets and events.

In buying early Lincolns, originality is crucial in establishing value. Lincoln enthusiasts are exceptionally knowledgeable on this subject. The Lincoln & Continental Owners Club has produced an *Authenticity Manual* for the 1940 through 1948 Continentals edited by Robert J. Prins. Reference to this guide is essential in establishing correctness of all parts of the car.

Chassis cards are available from Ford archives and are used as the final arbiter in disputes about authenticity. Judges are familiar with these cards and owners seeking perfection often obtain them by writing David Crippen, Ford Archives, P.O. Box 1970, Dearborn, Michigan, 48121.

Such a guide is especially crucial when facing a restored car. The money invested in a restoration is presumed recoverable by the seller, but if the restoration is not to standard, the investment is lost. The issue of correctness comes down to very fine detail. For example, on early Continentals interior work is more than correct cloth and leather; the stitching patterns on the seats must be considered along with correct beading, precise placement of cut-outs on carpeting, precise color on the instrument panel and so on. The use of gold finish was another specialty of the Continental; simply chroming at every point is unsatisfactory. Another example of a detail is the joint beneath the Continental windshield frame and the cowl. Occasionally an eager restorer will lead or bondo this joint.

The question of authenticity is also crucial on mechanical part finishes, plating and paint choice. For example, the trumpet horn screens are cadmium plated and the body of the horn is black, but the mounting bracket is car color and the bolt heads on the horn bracket are cadmium plated. It is on such detail that competent restorers measure a correct car. Woe to the restorer who starts chroming everything in sight or simply splashes black paint on everything. At the top of the market, the highest priced cars will conform to these standards.

The interchangeability of parts on Ford products produces pitfalls. Many substitutes will work, especially on such items as carburetors, generators and fuel pumps. A well-trained eye is essential in appraising a top restoration. For example, be on the lookout for an authentic Lincoln-Zephyr trademark on the side of the 1940–41 carburetor and the Zephyr name on the cylinder heads. Buyers seeking pristine cars would be well advised to attend some Lincoln Concours where experts can be observed in judging.

The rapidly growing appreciation for Lincolns of all ages comes from the realization that, in this great car, collectors find a rare combination of virtues. Buyers of Lincolns are in for happy motoring, good fellowship and the bonus of an appreciating market.

Paul R. Woudenberg
Pebble Beach, California

Chapter 1

1936–42 Lincoln-Zephyr and 1940–42 Lincoln Continental

★★★★★	Lincoln Continentals
★★★★★	Lincoln-Zephyr convertibles
★★★★	Limousines
★★★	Lincoln-Zephyr closed bodies

History

It was Edsel Ford with his usual foresight who placed an order with John Tjaarda in 1932 for the development of a radical prototype car. Tjaarda was a Dutch designer whose aircraft experience with Anthony Fokker had introduced him to aerodynamics in a way not typical of automotive engineers.

He had been hired by Ralph Roberts of the LeBaron studio, then part of the Briggs Company. Tjaarda's radical rear-engined car was completed in October of 1933 and shown in Detroit and then at the Century of Progress in Chicago in 1934. As a rear-engined car, it was hardly a commercial possibility for the Ford Motor Company, still

A late arrival in the high-dollar market is this 1938 Zephyr convertible sedan of which only 461 examples were made. Zephyrs were generally ignored amidst the popularity of the Continentals and most were junked. The fragility of the convertibles made them especially vulnerable. This splendid example, owned by Pat Ryan, is now worth more than the Continentals. *L.C.O.C.*

The second generation instrument panel of the 1938 Zephyr, highly stylized for the day. The gear shift is conventional but protrudes from behind the central console with a rod having several bends, all neatly hidden. The steering wheel is restrained. The great flat windshield offered a marvelous view of the road. The floor boards rose steeply at the firewall. Trim level was of the highest quality. *L.C.O.C.*

deeply conservative and ruled with an iron hand by the aging Henry Ford.

Under Edsel's inspiration, Eugene Turenne Gregorie Jr. skillfully transformed the Tjaarda prototype into a more conventional front-engined car, which became the 1936 Lincoln-Zephyr. The new twelve-cylinder engine was designed by Frank Johnson who was able to incorporate Ford V-8 engineering and low-cost production methods into a seventy-five-degree V block with the ancillaries mounted much like the Ford engine. The engine was very high revving with full power at 3900 rpm. More remarkable was a consistent torque figure of 180 lb-ft from 400 rpm to 3500 rpm which made the new Zephyr virtually a one-gear car. This 120 bhp engine coupled with a 3,300-pound car of unusual streamlining produced a 90 mph automobile. It was an instant success.

In September of 1938, Edsel ordered a special bodied Zephyr to be used for his winter vacation in Florida. He had just returned

Eugene T. Gregorie's mastery of the stream-lined idiom resulted in this superb 1939 Zephyr three-window coupe owned by Lloyd Pearson. The three-window coupe was introduced in 1937. The very long deck was a novelty even in 1939. Echoes of the 1939 Ford are clearly evi-

dent in the rear window shapes, the decklid, and the tail lamps but the added length of the Zephyr gives fresh grace to all of these components. These cars are now so rare that lucky owners are very reluctant to sell. Prices are rising. *L.C.O.C.*

from the Continent and asked Gregorie that the car be "Continental." It was ready by March 1939, in time for Edsel's use in Florida. The car was a sensation and Edsel at once saw production possibilities. A second prototype was ordered and in April, Edsel ordered production for the 1940 model year, naturally utilizing the new sheet metal of the 1940 model. On October 3 and October 6, 1939, the first two Lincoln Continental cabriolets were completed for the New York and Los Angeles shows. Twenty-five more were constructed in the last half of December. The first Continental coupe, H 101742, was completed on April 3, 1940, by which time 230 cabriolets had been constructed. Production V–12 engines were used with polished manifolds and chrome head nuts. The Columbia two-speed axle was fitted to 24 percent of production in 1940. A radio was chosen by 60 percent of buyers, hot air heater by 45 percent, white sidewall tires by 90 percent and chrome wheel bands by only 7 percent.

The strong response to the Continental prompted Lincoln to market it as a separate model line in 1941. A Warner overdrive was offered in 1941, fitted behind the transmission (code CAX on the production data card). The Columbia unit was also still available.

The Lincoln was restyled for 1942, and the Continental adopted the new boxy fenders and front end. The weight now was just over 4,000 pounds, and the V–12 was bored out one-sixteenth inch resulting in a 305 ci displacement producing 130 bhp. This modification began on January 6, 1942, and production ended on January 28; thus little experience was gained with the enlarged engine. When production resumed in 1945 approximately 1,797 engines were built to this dimension but the bore soon was reduced one-sixteenth inch to guard against cylinder wall weakness. Fifteen-inch wheels were used in 1942.

Another innovation for 1942 was the Liquamatic transmission, a cobbled response to General Motors' Hydra-matic. It was a combination of a vacuum-shifted three-speed transmission, an overdrive and a liquid coupling or fluid drive. In correct sequence, five forward gear ratios were possible. Even the

A front view of Lloyd Pearson's 1939 Zephyr coupe shows the new grille design with vertical bars, a theme which would continue through 1941. The oval wind wings are a charming accessory. New Zephyr bodies would appear in 1940, more bulky and perhaps not quite as graceful as these earlier models. *L.C.O.C.*

The 1940 Zephyr cabriolet was exceptionally clean in design. The grille bars were not surrounded and were much like the 1939 model. Extra bright work on the wheel trims makes for maximum impact. These cars have found great favor among collectors and continue to gain in value. L. D. Arrington is the owner of this fine car. *Tim Howley*

finest mechanic found it difficult to orchestrate the system and the company replaced the Liquamatics with conventional transmissions. No survivor has yet surfaced.

The 1942 Lincoln went on sale September 30, 1941. Government restrictions on the use of critical materials caused the end of aluminum heads in the fall of 1941; they had not been without service problems and the company was convinced that a change was necessary in any event. Compression of the iron heads was 7:1 rather than the aluminum 7.2:1. The production of chrome plating ended on December 15, 1941, except for functional areas such as bumpers. Existing stock of chrome items soon was exhausted. Blackout models began in January in which all brightwork was painted, even if plating had already been applied. Production stopped on February 2, 1942.

Prentice Bacon stands behind his 1941 Continental coupe. The rear quarter windows take away the claustrophobic feel of the Cabriolet interiors and as a comfortable four-passenger touring car, the coupe is hard to beat. The grille now is outlined by a chrome bar. Parking lamps are now mounted on top of the front fenders. Prices continue upward on this most handsome automobile. *L.C.O.C.*

1940 and 1941 Continental coupes stand side by side and offer a chance for comparison. The lighter colored 1941 on the right has the push-button door handles, the chrome outlined grille and parking lamps on the front fenders. Slight differences on the front bumpers may also be seen. *L.C.O.C.*

The Lincoln Custom was introduced in 1941 on a 138-inch wheelbase, a dimension set by the use of the standard drive shaft connected with the overdrive transmission. Normally the drive shaft used with overdrive was thirteen inches shorter. The big Zephyr club coupe doors were used. Rear doors were custom built based on Zephyr stampings. The Custom sedan weighed 4,150 pounds and the limousine 4,270 pounds. Prices were about the same as for the Continental, $2,550 for the sedan and $2,675 for the limousine.

Identification

The 1936 Zephyr was a startling design and is instantly recognized by the radical streamlined, rear fender skirts and a grille with horizontal lines which was copied in the 1937 Ford. Minor changes occurred in 1937, foremost of which were four bright

The 1941 Continental instrument panel is nicely balanced with the important instruments directly in front of the driver. Continental quality was evident in these handsome gauges and fine die-cast work in the grille. The neat latching system for the top reflects Ford's long experience in building convertibles. *L.C.O.C.*

pairs of grille bars spaced evenly through the height of the grille. The little side louvers on the hood were made narrower.

In 1938, the Zephyr grille was set low in the front of the car and fitted with horizontal louvers with a metal outline, a trend setting design not only for Lincoln but for the whole industry. The same theme was used in 1939 with vertical bars.

The new body was introduced in 1940, bulkier than the original 1936 design. The grille was virtually unchanged but sealed beams lamps were now fitted. The hub cap script read "Lincoln-Zephyr." The hood ornament, a ball with horizontal pod, turned to open the hood.

In 1941, the body was unchanged but there were many trim differences. Parking lamps were now mounted on the crown of the front fender. The hub caps read "Lincoln V–12." The door latches were push button. The chrome grille was outlined by a chrome surround. The hood ornament was stationary and the release was now under the dash.

For 1942, new boxy fenders were applied to the unchanged body shell. The grille was now a massive affair with fine horizontal bars, and a bulky lower extension, also with fine bars. The hood ornament was a ball with a vertical blade.

Serial numbers
1936—H1 to H15,528
1937—H15,529 to H45,529
1938—H45,530 to H64,640
1939—H64,641 to H85,640
1940—H85,641 to H107,687
1941—H107,688 to H129,690
1942—H129,621 to H136,254

A very rare 1941 Lincoln Custom limousine with glass division. The 138 inch wheelbase was achieved by the use of the standard long drive-shaft connected with the overdrive transmission. On standard-length cars with the overdrive, a 13 inch shorter driveshaft was fitted. The car was heavy at 4,270 pounds and the V–12 engine had its work cut out for it. Very few of these cars have survived of the original low production of only 295. For collectors interested in the unusual, this car has special appeal. *L.C.O.C.*

Colors

In 1940, the standard Zephyr and Continental colors were:

	Continental cabriolets	Continental coupes
Black	123	19
Dove gray	25	1
Beetle (spode) green	24	3
Zephyr blue	31	6
Burgundy red	42	6
Ardun green poly	9	3
Eagle gray poly	3	
Capri blue poly	45	6
Tropical sand poly	25	4
Stanhope green	2	

Special colors

Bennington gray	5	2
Benton gray	1	
Cotswold gray		1
Cigarette cream (Model A color?)	2	1
Croydon cream	1	
Italian cream	1	
White enamel	1	
Salon pink	2	2
Luxrite copper	1	
Cherokee red (Frank Lloyd Wright)	1	
Oxblood maroon	1	
Special blue	1	
Special blue #2	1	
Special blue MX 900268	1	
Lyon blue	1	
Monterey iridescent blue	1	

Of the 400 Continental cabriolets in 1941, 116 were painted black, according to research by Lincoln & Continental Owners Club member Steve Hastings. Forty-five tu-tone combinations are also listed for coupes, as compiled by club member H. H. Nutting.

Regular colors	Single color cabriolets	Add for coupe tu-tones	
Black	116	Plympton gray poly	1
Plympton gray poly	57	Sea mist gray metallic	12
Darian blue poly	48	Rockingham tan	1
Paradise green	44	Spode green	2
Zephyr blue	42	Cape Cod gray	4
Spode green	35	Darian blue	1
Volanta coach maroon	23	Staffordshire green or	13
Rockingham tan	13	Plympton gray poly	1
Dimonte blue metallic	4	Curacáo brown	5
Lancaster green metallic	4	Sea mist gray metallic	1
Special colors	14		
Total cabriolets for 1941	400		

Capri blue metallic also was used for 1941 coupes.

If standard colors in combination were not enough, a 1941 coupe customer could order

The 1942 Lincoln production ended on February 2. Only 200 of these Continental coupes were built. The new boxy fenders combined with a very massive grille (with fine horizontal bars) to give the Continental a new look, especially harmonious when combined with the Coupe's angular upper body. The 1942 models have found a special following among collectors. *L.C.O.C.*

13

In 1936, the great Model K sold a grand total of about 1,500 units of which eight were this beautiful seven passenger touring. Production would collapse in 1937 and 1938. Edsel Ford rightly sensed that the K was not only unprofitable but had no future, spurring him to introduce the Zephyr in 1936. It arrived just in time and saved the company. *Ford Motor Company*

This straight profile photo of the 1940 Lincoln Continental shows the superb balance of this design. There was nothing like it on the American market and it instantly captured the notice of the esthetically minded cognoscenti. *Ford Motor Company*

virtually any color to personal taste and twenty-one customers did just that. Two of these special colors were used on two cars. Even then, two more customers ordered their cars in primer.

Cabriolets did not normally lend themselves to tu-tone combinations but one cabriolet was delivered with a Plympton gray body and black fenders.

It is clear that both the 1940 and 1941 Continental were offered in a rainbow of colors. When preparing for top competition in a Lincoln Concours, it is not enough simply to pick any of the standard or even special colors. The object is originality, so a color choice is usually backed up with a copy of the original body card which will justify the precise color chosen. If such competition is not the primary objective, the many choices above should provide ample scope for choosing a color or colors once used on a new Lincoln.

Production

1936 Zephyr	
4–dr sedan	12,272
Export	908
2–dr sedan	1,814
Total	14,994

1937 Zephyr	
4–dr sedan	23,159
2–dr coupe sedan	1,500
3–passenger coupe	5,199
Town limousine	139
Total	29,997

1938 Zephyr	
4–dr sedan	14,520
3–passenger coupe	2,600
2–dr coupe sedan	800
4–dr conv. sedan	461
3–passenger conv. coupe	600
Town limousine	130
Total	19,111

1939 Zephyr	
4–dr sedan	16,663
2–dr coupe sedan	800
3–passenger coupe	2,500
4–dr conv. sedan	302
3–passenger conv. coupe	640
Total	20,905

This lovely factory photo captures the highlights of the 1940 Continental cabriolet. Apart from the fender stampings, the body was pretty much hand built which, even in those low-labor-cost days, doubled the price over the Lincoln sedan. *Ford Motor Company*

Production

1940 Zephyr and Continental

4-dr sedan	15,764
5-passenger coupe	316
3-passenger coupe	1,256
Convertible coupe	700
Club coupe	3,500
Continental cabriolet	350
Continental club coupe	54
7-passenger custom limousine	4
Custom town car	4
Total	21,948

1941 Zephyr and Continental

4-dr sedan	14,469
5-passenger club coupe	3,750
3-passenger coupe	972
5-passenger coupe	178
Convertible	725
Continental cabriolet	450
Continental coupe	400
Custom 4-dr, 7-passenger sedan (138-inch wheelbase)	355
Custom limousine (138-inch wheelbase)	295
Total	22,994

1942 Zephyr and Continental

4-dr sedan	4,412
Club coupe	1,236
3-passenger coupe	273
Convertible	191
Continental cabriolet	136
Continental coupe	200
Custom 7-passenger sedan	47
Custom 7-passenger limousine	295
Specials	2
Total	6,792

Some firsts

1940 Continental cabriolet: Prototype H85,825 built October 3, 1939 and prototype H86,025 built October 10, 1939. Production began December 13, 1939

1940 coupe: Prototype H101,742 built April 3, 1940. Production began May 27, 1940 through July 8, 1940.

1941 Continental cabriolet: Production began August 2, 1940 with H107,689.

1941 Continental coupe: Production began August 5, 1940 with H107,690.

Problem areas

By 1940, the Zephyr V-12 engine had become quite reliable, but they are sensitive to problems caused by blow-by past worn rings. As engines built up mileage, the rings allowed blow-by at ignition firing creating fumes in the crankcase. When the amount of blow-by is small, it is easily sucked up a small pipe connecting the top of the crankcase to the air cleaner. The fumes then passed down through the carburetor and into the combustion chamber where they would be burned unnoticed amidst general oil consumption passing up by the rings. Fresh air entered at the rear oil filler pipe which would cleanse the area and pass up the small pipe.

With further wear, increasing blow-by created pressure in the crankcase, overwhelming the rear oil filler pipe. Fresh air no longer entered the rear oil filler; instead fumes exited and often were wafted into the passenger compartment. Oil could even be driven up the fuel pump tower or past the rear main bearing. In a very worn engine, even the fuming at the oil filler can be guided into the air cleaner with appropriate pipe work, a trick used by weary owners but hardly recommended. When buying a Lincoln of this era, look for oil leaks, condensation of fumes and general oily grime in the engine compartment. Also, warm up the engine and check the oil pressure. It should be at least ten pounds.

Sometimes a manifold gasket is installed with no precut hole to allow fumes to be sucked into the air cleaner. The small pipe itself may be missing and the hole blocked to stop fuming. This only makes things worse. Check that all the parts are in place and working.

There is a substantial amount of literature on trouble-shooting a Columbia two-speed axle. Perhaps this is an ominous sign but in general these units are reliable. Check for easy shifting, consistent operation and noise.

The big ninety-pound doors on these Continentals can sag, caused either by a breakdown of the door metal usually around the lower hinge or a deterioration of the door post. Door weakness will be revealed in cracks indicating that the welds have broken

Kermit Wilson's beautiful 1942 Custom limousine is a super rare car. 295 were built, no doubt in anticipation of World War II, and very few have survived. The trim and finish is superb. *Grady Jacoway*

loose or rust has compromised the door structure. Aluminum castings inside the body post support the hinges on the prewar cars and can deteriorate to the point where the hinge bolts will no longer hold. If either problem is present, be prepared for heavy reconstruction costs. Restorers favor the 1946–48 iron door post castings, if they can be found. Problems in the door area will also suggest a close inspection of floor panels and all sheet metal exposed to road spray.

Camshaft wear is not unknown on the V–12 engine and will produce a rough-running, low-powered engine. Regrinding is possible on the original cast iron cams; the cast cams are often porous and have limited life.

Market history

At the close of the war in July 1945, the average price of the 1941 Continental club coupe was $3,853, 137 percent of the 1941 base price of $2,811. Wartime inflation had pushed used car prices up against the Government's Office of Price Administra-tion (OPA) ceilings. These ceilings had been instituted in 1942 to control inflation.

A year later, Kelly Blue Book retail prices were slipping below the OPA ceilings. The 1941 coupe had dropped to $3,100 and the cabriolet to $3,200. In 1947 the price had fallen sharply to $1,585 for the coupe and $1,700 for the cabriolet. In 1949 the price for both coupe and cabriolet was $1,395. By 1952 the price of the 1941 Continental was around $400 and would no longer appear in the commercial used car guides.

Prewar Continentals were available for near junk prices through the fifties. By 1960 the average price for a prewar Continental was around $1,000 with best examples at perhaps $1,500. Collectibility began in the sixties and values climbed slowly. In 1966, a cabriolet in need of upholstery and top could still be bought for $650 with other better cars offered at $1,450 to $2,200. By 1970 the 1940–41 Continentals were well rediscov-ered and good examples were bringing $5,000 or more. One eager enthusiast wrote a letter to the editor of *Continental Comments* in the fall of 1971 and noted that the cars had

The famous Presidential parade car, Sunshine Special, a 1939 Model K with 1942 front grille and sheet metal. The conversion is neatly done. This car was armor plated and weighed 9,300 pounds. *Ford Motor Company*

appreciated 200 percent in two years, which led him to predict a value of $10,000 by 1973. He was on the right track but it took about six years more. By 1978, the 1940 Continental coupe had a top value of around $12,000. The cabriolet was 50 percent higher.

The prices moved upward quickly. In 1982 the top prices for the 1940–41 coupes were around $20,000, and the cabriolets were still at a 50 percent premium of $30,000. In the eighties, the appreciation was slower, and by the end of 1987 top prices were $30,000 for 1940 coupes with an auction price of $36,000 for a superb original cabriolet. The 1941s were 10 percent cheaper. Recent appreciation has been more rapid, and at the beginning of 1989 the coupes were at $36,000 and the cabriolets at $42,000.

The Zephyr cabriolets were "discovered" in the sixties and it soon was recognized that they had survived in smaller numbers than the Continentals. Production had been low and there were just 700 of the 1940 and 725 of the 1941 cabriolets. Many had already been lost. Prices were initially much lower than the Continentals but have tended in recent years to stabilize just slightly below the Continental coupes and cabriolets.

Substantial appreciation has taken place in the closed Zephyr models. In 1978, closed Zephyrs were selling for under $10,000, generally about one-half of the Continental cabriolet prices. This relationship has remained roughly the same through the eighties and into the nineties.

The following table summarizes the top retail price history of the 1940 and 1941 Continentals. The quotes come from various sources and represent good to excellent cars. Prices are approximate for both years; the 1941 sometimes sold for slightly less. The 1942 models were at a slight premium.

1945—$3,853 (OPA ceiling price)
1946—$3,200 (Kelley Blue Book)
1947—$1,700 (Kelley Blue Book)
1949—$1,395 (Kelley Blue Book)
1952—$400 (a low point—many cars being junked)
1954—$750
1957—$1,000

1959—$1,200 (many cars below $1,000 with nonstock engines)
1962—$1,500
1965—$2,300
1970—$5,000
1975—$9,000
1977—$12,000
1979—$18,000 (general inflation)
1982—$30,000
1984—$30,000 (Old Cars Price Guide)
1986—$32,000
1987—$36,000
1988—$37,000
1989—$42,000
1990—$60,000

The table shows that the market moves in steps interspersed with plateaus of price consolidation. The various price guides are revised at intervals and do not always reflect a steady market. Exceptional sales at auctions may distort the perceptions of market values.

It must be added that many of the prewar cars available in the fifties were in poor shape with substitute V–8 engines and other indignities. After 1980 more and more cars were being brought into top condition, since restoration costs were justified by rising prices. Good cars in turn accelerate rising prices. By the year 2000 there should be virtually no unrestored cars left.

There is another factor in establishing market trends. As is the case with the prewar Ford market, the average age of prewar Continental owners continues to climb which inevitably means that these cars will often be placed on the open market as owners move on to the "great garage in the sky." Will the availability of some of these cars serve to restrain upward prices? Probably not, because the number of cars available is so low. Unlike older Fords, the prewar Zephyrs have shown substantially sharp appreciation since 1985. There may be some crossover of Ford enthusiasts into this Lincoln market.

In approximate terms, prices of prewar Continentals have tended to double in every decade with exception of the period 1970–80 when prices tripled. If this trend were to continue, the price of a fine 1940–41 Continental would be about $80,000 at the year

2000. Recent trends suggest that the decade 1990–2000 may be a hyper market time for all collectibles; if that is the case, the Continental in the year 2000 may be in the $100,000 to $120,000 area as a low estimate and perhaps $300,000 to $500,000 as a high estimate. These prices may seem ridiculous in 1990 but the fact that the Continental was one of the few great American world-class cars of the 1940s argues for a bold estimate. All Zephyr prices should be helped by such market advances of the Continental. The faithful preservation of Continentals by club members and enthusiasts has helped to maintain a good pool of cars. New younger buyers are discovering the early Continentals, but rising prices make youthful entry into this market increasingly difficult.

Of the prewar Zephyrs, one style, the 1938–39 convertible sedan, has now nearly matched the Continentals in sheer value. Only 461 were built in 1938 and 302 in 1939; a handful remain. Likewise Zephyr cabriolets are now much sought after. In truth, Zephyrs of any year, other than four-door sedans, are exceptionally rare.

The prewar Continental market should remain strong through the nineties, providing great owner satisfaction with sound, perhaps even spectacular, investment returns. The Zephyr market may have additional upward volatility as these rare cars find wider appreciation.

Suggested reading

Issue #133 of *Continental Comments* provides fifty-nine pictures of engine and chassis details to be considered when restoring a 1940 Continental. This splendid presentation is by Lloyd Erick Pearson. Another fine restoration article by Seymour Petrovsky has twenty-seven more pictures to aid in restoration (#164 *Continental Comments*). Dave Cole writes a lengthy and erudite piece on the location and direction of the thermostats in the radiator hoses! (#164) The standards are very high.

Further information on paint color may be found in the *Authenticity Manual for the Lincoln Zephyr* by Robert J. Prins, and *Continental Comments* #140, Spring 1980, and #156, Second Quarter 1984.

A row of Zephyrs. Roy Thorson's 1937 three-window coupe is on the left. In the center is Bob Francy's 1939 three-window coupe, flanked by his 1942 convertible. All of these cars are exceptionally rare. There may be only four 1942 convertibles remaining. *L.C.O.C.*

★★★★★	Lincoln Continental convertibles
★★★★	Lincoln Continental coupes
★★★	Lincolns

1946–48 Lincoln and Lincoln Continental

History

Production of the 1946 Lincoln and Lincoln Continental began on November 1, 1945, and by the end of the year 569 units had been assembled. The new car was announced on January 6, 1946. The new heavy eggcrate grille had been designed five years before in 1941 by Gregorie to fit directly into the new 1942 model sheet metal. The design was in tune with the times and resembled the 1946 Cadillac.

In almost all respects the 1946 car was identical to the 1942 model. The three-window coupe was dropped but the sedan, club coupe and convertible coupe remained. The two Continental styles were unchanged.

The 305 ci engine was fitted to early production through engine number H138,052.

The 1946 Lincoln four-door sedan, a very early model built in late 1945 as evidenced by the lack of fog lamps. The 1942 body sheet metal is reproduced without change. The new "mouth organ" grille, very heavy in design and dominating the car, echoes 1942 Cadillac themes. The outward flare at the bottom of the doors gives the car a somewhat "squatty" appearance. Collectors usually prefer more sporting body styles. *Ford Motor Company*

Cylinder wall thickness was found to be unreliable on this engine so the bore was reduced $\frac{1}{16}$ inch restoring the 1941 wall thickness. With the reduced bore, engine compression went up slightly. Horsepower was still continued at 125, but now at 4000 rpm instead of 3600 rpm. Torque dropped from 235 lbs-ft at 1800 rpm on the 305 ci engine to 214 lbs-ft at 1600 rpm on the 292 ci engine.

The cabriolet weighed about 4,525 pounds when professionally tested in 1947 and would accelerate from zero to 60 mph in 21.6 seconds. The horsepower peak was reached at 78 mph and the approximate top speed was 87 mph, very good considering that weight. The brakes were a weak point and fade began under test after four applications of bringing the car speed from 60 mph to 30 mph. Gasoline mileage in the city was about 10 mpg but, with prudent driving and overdrive, could reach 15 mpg over the road.

The 1946 Lincoln and Continental sold strongly in a car starved market, and there were virtually no changes for the 1947 and 1948 model years. Production concluded on March 24, 1948, after a grand total of 45,574 cars had been built.

Identification

The 1946 hubcaps had the word "Lincoln" set in block letters in an octagon. The hood ornament was a ball with twin upright blades. Wheel trim rings had three ribs. For 1947 "Lincoln" appeared in script on the hubcap. Wider plain wheel rim rings were introduced in mid 1947 as was the hood ornament, a ball with a single vertical blade. There were virtually no changes for the 1948 models.

Serial numbers

Continental production used chassis numbers in random sequence for production. Cars were often delivered out of order.
1946—H136255 to H152839
1947—7H152840 to 7H174289
1948—8H174290 to 8H182129

Colors

Bob Petrucelli (a club member) has assembled the following information on paint. "Opal" means opalescent, added to the formula. The eight standard colors for the Continental in 1946 and early 1947 were:
Black
Lincoln maroon (same as 1942 Victoria
    coach maroon)
Sheldon gray opal (same name as 1942 but
    slightly different shade)
Skyline blue opal
Surf green opal
Willow green
Marine blue
Wing gray
Special Colors
Lincoln maroon metallic

In January, 1946, the fog lamp was introduced in the front grille and a kit for retrofitting the lamps was made available. The early cover plate is laid out on the white paper on the left. *Ford Motor Company*

The Continental in its first postwar guise used the new bold grille to advantage and focuses attention on the front of the car. The lower grille work blends with the bumper creating an unusually aggressive effect. *Ford Motor Company*

This handsome picture of Wally Williamson's 1946 cabriolet is set off by the palm lined street in Fort Lauderdale. It is easy to understand why these cars were so popular when new and why their value continues to soar. *Tim Howley*

The rear trunk on this 1948 Continental was one of the keys to the styling mastery of the great car. The added height of the trunk set off the lowness of the body; the bulk at the rear emphasized litheness in the rest of the body. These themes were continued on the later Mark series and were widely copied. It is an idea that has found fresh favor in the eighties and nineties. Tom Lerch is the owner of this car. *Tim Howley*

This handsome 1948 Continental coupe is nicely set off by the two tone paint job. Though production ended very early, 846 coupes were built, a record for the three postwar years of Continental production. Over 147 of these coupes are listed in the club registry. Alex Lewis owns this car. *Tim Howley*

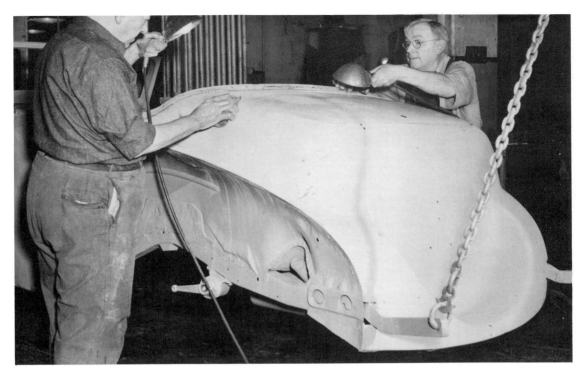

The 1946 Lincoln Continental, like its predecessors, required a lot of handwork. Here workmen hand sand the rear trunk area. A look in the wheel arch reveals that the body was welded directly to the frame. The lack of tooling made the Continental an expensive car to build. *Ford Motor Company*

Lizard green metallic
Russet brown metallic
Silver green
Storm cloud
Storm gray metallic
Beginning in April 1947, the thirteen
    standard colors were:
Black
Maroon (same as 1942 Victoria coach
    maroon)
Moss green
Grotto blue
Steel gray metallic opal
Pace car yellow (not used on coupes)
Shell gray (not used on coupes)
Sea gull gray
Dune beige
Canyon tan (not used on coupes)
Regal blue
Valley green metallic opal
Opal blue green

Here is a 1946 Continental coupe which demonstrates the new harmony of the post-war grille with the original body contours. The squared-off fender lines work especially well with the angular greenhouse. K. R. Posey owns this car. *Tim Howley*

Special Colors
Pearl paint beginning 6/47 (four-door sedan)
Krimmer gray beginning 7/47 (four-door sedan)
River mist beginning 7/47
Lido green metallic beginning 10/47

Production

1946	Lincoln	16,179
	Continental coupes	265
	Continental cabriolets	201
	Total	16,645

1947	Lincoln	19,891
	Continental coupes	831
	Continental cabriolets	738
	Total	21,460

1948	Lincoln	6,170
	Continental coupes	847
	Continental cabriolets	452
	Total	7,469

Early 1947 Continentals from H152,840 to H154,096 are identical to 1946.

The first 1947 coupe was H152906, completed on January 31, 1947.

The last 1947 coupe was H173953.

On October 28, 1947, the first (1948) production coupe was completed.

On March 24, 1948, the last day of production, two production coupes were produced, H182,032 and H181,093.

Dr. John L. Mansell, a club member, has documented five movie studios and some noted personalities who bought Continentals:

H139,428: Built Apr. 7, 1946 for 20th Century Fox
H140,916: Built July 24, 1946 for Warner Brothers
H141,036: Built July 29, 1946 for MGM
H139,514: Built Aug. 14, 1946 for Universal
H143,328: Built Sept. 24, 1946 for Columbia
H147,990: Built Nov. 21, 1946 for Jack Benny
H143,173: Built Aug. 30, 1946 for Bob Hope
H147,286: Built Nov. 1946 for Greer Garson
H148,972: Built Dec. 1946 for Harry Wismer
H149,234: Built Dec. 1946 for Jimmy Durante

An oddity. This 1946 Custom Limousine was not cataloged and there is no evidence of production. It may well be a 1942 which has been updated. The heavy duty truck wheels suggest heavy armor plating. The red light, grab handles on the A pillar and on the trunk, and flag standard point to Federal service. Yet where are the step plates? *Ford Motor Company*

Problem areas

Look for free play in the steering wheel of the 1946–48 models which may be traced to a loose Pitman arm. The big nut has a cotter pin which suggests that the whole unit is dead tight but the splines can wear. Any motion at the spline is much magnified. Check carefully for any play.

It has been noted that the bore was reduced to 2⅞ inches in 1946 as wall thickness was observed to be unreliable. Despite this there are some owners who have bored out the V–12 engine to three inches (318 ci) and even to 3¹/₁₆ inches (331 ci). OCee Ritch in his 1963 book, *The Lincoln Continental*, reckoned a 12.5 percent cylinder wall failure rate with this large bore, but that was in 1961. As these engines age, interior corrosion further weakens cylinder walls and the chance of reliability is diminished with overbore. Avoid buying a Lincoln that has been overbored.

Oil consumption is always a problem with an aging engine. Sometimes the manifold gasket is not perforated over the center of the engine and crankcase fumes are unable to pass up the little tube to the air cleaner and then into the carburetor. Air is supposed to flow into the crankcase through the filler cap and then is drawn through the tube into the carburetor air cleaner and then through the combustion chambers. The developing blow-by soon creates crankcase pressure which overwhelms the slight carburetor-produced vacuum; this smoke emerges from the filler cap causing dirt and grime on the firewall. Higher vacuum can be found below the carburetor; this could be used by tapping a line and drawing fumes with a restricted flow, but at the risk of leaning the mixture, disturbing carburetion and maybe burning valves. Gas heater exhaust plates used beneath the carburetor can be used in this way to draw fumes but they are now very rare.

Buyers should thus be on the lookout for a dirty engine compartment, which betrays evidence of oil fume blow-by. It might be useful to watch for a recently cleaned engine compartment with oil residues in crevices.

Market history

The postwar Continentals were highly valued from the beginning and showed remarkable price retention. In the fall of 1949, a 1946 Continental could command $2,200, about 50 percent of the original price. By 1955, the V–12 Lincoln prices had virtually descended to junk value; in 1956, *Continental Comments* urged Lincoln collectors to scout for junk 1946–48 Lincolns available at $50 to $100 for valuable parts for Continentals. But the Continentals were still selling at prices from $1,000 to $1,800. By 1960, the average asking price had risen to around $2,000.

Enthusiasts began restoring the prewar Continentals in the sixties which helped the value of the 1946–48 models, though they were initially seen as "second best." By the mid-sixties, the 1946–48 market was spotty with prices for ordinary specimens beginning as low as $600 and going up to a top of about $2,500. During the seventies the appreciation of Continentals was underway in earnest, and by 1976 prices for good 1946–1948s had passed $10,000. Prices climbed very steeply during the inflationary times around 1980 so that by 1982, postwar Continental convertibles were between $25,000 and $30,000, with coupes about $17,000. The market remained flat through the mid-eighties and then began a steep climb in 1987.

Auctions stimulated the Continental market. A superb 1947 convertible reached $53,000 at Newport Beach in July 1988, but many convertibles in condition #2 (a fine well-restored car or extremely well-maintained original) were sold in the $20,000 region. The coupe auction prices are lower, with condition #2 prices normally in the $15,000 to $20,000 area. Sellers will usually overestimate the condition of their car (just as buyers will usually underestimate). But buyers should beware that a peak auction price, especially at one of the national venues which seem to be on the west coast or at Scottsdale, Arizona, may not represent the true market value.

The bottom of the Continental market is about $6,000, usually for a rough car often with a nonstock engine and needing much work. Buyers seeking bargains here should remember the high cost of restoration which will usually not repay the investment. Costs can be offset by home restoration, which perhaps is the real point of the hobby! Hats off to the skilled restorer-owner.

The 1946–48 Continental has now caught up in value with the 1940–42 models. Perhaps it is its massive, dramatic appearance which has found favor. The boxy style has aged far more gracefully than early purists committed to the prewar style may have believed.

The nineties should see continued appreciation of the 1946–48 models. Strong club support and good parts availability make these cars attractive prospects for the owner-driver, while speculators are drawn by the flamboyant style, and the availability remains good since few of these cars were ever voluntarily junked.

Another factor contributing to value is that the early postwar cars have special appeal to collectors born in the thirties who have now reached a moment in life when they can indulge youthful dreams. It is the high school memories which often dominate.

It is also possible that the Ford collectors see the Continental as a target car, a rich but manageable cousin whose technical familiarity gives reassurance.

The 1946–48 Continental is the final statement of the Edsel Ford and the "old company" and is a tribute to his creative genius. It retains all of the idiosyncrasies of the early cars and also the charm and pleasures. Collectors will continue to be drawn to these splendid cars and their future prospects remain bright.

Jim Malone's 1947 cabriolet looks especially handsome when set off against the dark shadow of the hotel entrance. These fine cars have found a large following among collectors and prices have risen steeply in the eighties. Prospects continue strong for the nineties. *Tim Howley*

| ★★★★★ | Convertibles |
| ★★★ | All others |

1949–51 Cosmopolitan and Lincoln

History

The 1949 Lincoln was the last design of E. T. Gregorie, the gifted Ford stylist who had played such an important role in the development of the Zephyr. Gregorie had a turbulent career in the forties. The declining strength of Henry Ford after 1941 and the tragic death of Edsel Ford on May 26, 1943, opened up a power vacuum in the company which was filled by Harry Bennett. Bennett, a tough hatchet man who had been with the company since 1915, quickly dominated affairs. In 1943, A. M. Wibel, one of the most able financial men in the company, was fired along with Laurence Sheldrick, the engineer who developed the 1932 V–8. Gregorie soon

The 1949 Lincoln shared body dies with the Mercury. The big 152 bhp V–8 engine, however, put the Lincoln in a higher performance class. These small Lincolns have not survived in any numbers and finding one today is very difficult. This beautiful example is owned by Bob Shifler. *L.C.O.C.*

The handsome lines of the 1949 Lincoln flowed all the way to the rear bumper. *L.C.O.C.*

Even rarer than the Lincoln four door is this 1949 two-door convertible, built for only this year. Again the body is shared with the Mercury and a particularly handsome style it was. It is hard to estimate a price for this car because only three or four are known to exist. *L.C.O.C.*

was dismissed. And in April of 1944, the mighty production genius Charles Sorensen was gone.

Alone among these pioneers, Gregorie was to return in late 1944 and again pick up the styling duties. He had been working on strikingly new designs from 1941 to 1943, the clays of which would strongly resemble the 1949 models. No one yet knew what the timetable would be for new models, but as the war continued it became clear that delays were inevitable. By June 1945, Gregorie had produced a clay virtually identical to the 1949 Cosmopolitan.

These time frames are important because Gregorie's 1949 Lincoln styling themes were perhaps seven years old by the time the car was introduced. Both General Motors and Chrysler designs were moving toward more angularity which would appear in 1949 and 1950 and which would accentuate the dated look of Lincoln and Mercury products.

Development proceeded quickly in 1945. A new big V-8 engine was laid out under the direction of C. C. Johnson with a bore and stroke of 3½ by 4⅜ inches to produce a displacement of 337 ci. This "EQ" block followed standard Ford practice and was tough and heavy, well able to power the Ford F7 and F8 truck line when it was introduced in January of 1948. The engine produced 152 bhp on a 7.1:1 compression ratio at 3600 rpm. Torque was 254 lb-ft at 1800 rpm, well up from the V-12's 225 lb-ft. Announcement of this engine for Lincoln use came on February 24, 1948. The benefits of development in truck service plus interchangeability of parts promised reliability.

The engine was mated to a conventional transmission with a 1.581 second gear and a 2.526 low gear. The absence of an automatic transmission was a serious problem since 97 percent of all Cadillacs in 1948 had Hydramatic. Harold Youngren, now on the Ford

Here is what happened to so many 1949 Lincolns; junking began in the late fifties. To Lincoln collectors, discovering a 1949 Lincoln convertible like this would be the equivalent of finding the Holy Grail. This car is clearly restorable and would be worth an enormous sum when finished. Could there yet be some of these cars still in wrecking yards? *Tim Howley*

The splendid "EQ" Lincoln V-8 engine displaced 337 ci and produced 152 bhp on a 7.1 compression ratio at 3600 bhp. Torque was 254 pounds feet at 1800 rpm, a 15% improvement on the V-12. It was designed by C. C. Johnson and was introduced in January 1948 in the F7 and F8 truck line. It was announced as the Lincoln engine in February. It followed standard Ford V-8 L-head design and was a tough engine. It lifted speed of the Lincoln to 102 mph, at the time the only American car that could exceed 100 mph. *Ford Archives, Henry Ford Museum*

team, had hoped that his old firm of Borg-Warner might help but they had nothing available. After June 26, 1949, the Hydramatic was offered on the Lincoln, an embarrassing admission of GM leadership. Tires were 8.20x15.

Two distinct new models were presented, the Cosmopolitan and the Lincoln. The smaller Lincoln shared the body shell of the Mercury, a design which Gregorie had originally planned for the Ford. This 118-inch wheelbase car was rejected in the summer of 1946 by Ernest Breech, the new vice president, as being too big for a Ford, and on September 3, 1946, it became the new 1949 Mercury and, on a 121-inch wheelbase, the new small Lincoln. The Lincoln was 623 pounds heavier, much of this weight being in the engine. It was a handsome car with a relatively small "greenhouse" which gave it a racy appearance.

Gregorie designed the Cosmopolitan as a Lincoln but the June 1945 clay mock-up had a Mercury grille. It became the top-of-the-line Lincoln on a 125-inch wheelbase for 1949. The Cosmopolitan in sedan form

By 1951, Lincoln had added rudimentary rear fender blades. The grille had been modified and the quality level was very high. These cars are very hard to find now and the absence of examples has made it difficult to form a cadre of enthusiasts. *Ford Motor Company*

weighed 4,249 pounds, three hundred pounds more than a Cadillac 62.

The new Lincoln and Cosmopolitan were introduced on April 22, 1948, the first of the 1949 model cars, which delighted Lincoln dealers. For the first time, the Lincoln could go head to head against the luxury competition, especially a competition which, with the exception of the new Cadillac, was selling 1946-style automobiles. The new cars

The 1949 Cosmopolitan was a smooth car, a statement of stylist Gregorie's rounded style. It was compared unfavorably to the new angularity of the GM cars. History has a way of vindicating some ideas and the rounded Fords of the mid eighties conquered GM angularity. The Cosmopolitan was 220 inches long and the convertible, at 4,505 pounds was the heaviest body style. It was a big fast car with good road manners. Collectors today rate this car very highly and prices are continuing to climb. *Ford Motor Company*

The 1950 Cosmopolitan four door Sport sedan had a redesigned grille to obliterate Gregorie's "frowning" grille. The design was better in many respects and the car was much improved mechanically. The great curving surfaces brought forth irreverent comments about "beached whales." The dated styling of Gregorie's work, done in the early forties, was all too evident. Production totaled 8,341, minuscule by present day standards. This is one reason why these cars are not easy to find. *Ford Motor Company*

1951 Cosmopolitan styling was even better than 1950. The big chrome slash stripe over the front wheel arch was removed and replaced with a long side spear. The grille was further simplified and the car was more elegant in its restraint. The market responded positively as 12,229 of these Sport sedans were sold, a fine showing for the third year of a dated design. Few have survived. *Ford Motor Company*

Only 857 Cosmopolitan convertibles were sold in 1951 and this one belongs to Cal and Nancy Beauregard. By 1951, the Cosmopolitan was a very refined car and provided luxurious high-speed touring. Prices for this very rare model will be high. *Tim Howley*

were fast, both the Lincoln and the Cosmopolitan could touch 102 mph, the only American cars able to exceed 100 mph.

For 1950, the Lincoln was much improved. The door locks were new, fiberglass was added to the firewall to reduce heat flow, the steering column was isolated by rubber to reduce squeaks, the heat and controls were new, and many control systems were redesigned. Of more fundamental importance was a redesign of the choke to stop Hydramatic creep and improved balancing of the engine, done mid-year, to stop vibration. The car was much more "finished" with such detail items as an upholstered center door pillar instead of a plain metal. 8.00x15 tires were used on the Lincoln while 8.20x15 continued on the Cosmopolitan.

Though Lincoln called the regular four-door sedan a Sport sedan from 1949 to 1951, there was nothing especially sporty about the design. The Cadillac DeVille in 1949 and the Chrysler Windsor Newport in 1950 were hardtop coupes and represented a new styling trend. Lincoln could only answer with a specially trimmed coupe in both lines called the Lincoln Lido and the Cosmopoli-

tan Capri, introduced in July 5, 1950. These cars had padded tops and vivid interiors.

Lincoln speed drew racing enthusiasts. In the first Mexican Road Race, Johnny Mantz finished ninth.

The 1951 Lincoln and Cosmopolitan were announced on November 15, 1950. The grille was restyled and the 1949 "frown" was modified. Small rear fender extensions appeared, a concession to the Cadillac fin styling. Numerous luxury options were offered and the refinement of all components was evident. The Lincoln was a great car, capable of 100 mph yet able to produce 25 mpg on the Mobilgas Economy Run on March 8, 1951. Horsepower was slightly up in 1951 to 154.

A series of 1949–50 Lincolns were used in government service. Ten were ordered for the White House and nine for other VIP uses. A 145-inch wheelbase was used on all nineteen cars. Eighteen were limousines constructed by Henney Motor Company in Freeport, Illinois. The remaining car was an open-top parade car constructed by Ray Dietrich in Grand Rapids, Michigan. As a presidential special it was given disappearing

This 1950 Presidential limousine is typical of those used by the White House. These very special custom built cars have found a market niche among collectors, but only a handful are available. The quality level was superb. The weight of these cars exceeds 6,000 pounds but the big "EQ" V-8 engine did a remarkable job in handling the load. *Ford Motor Company*

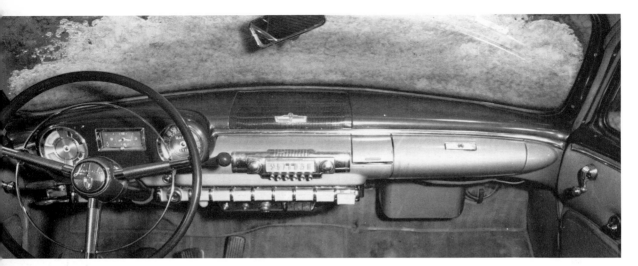

The instrument panel of the 1949 Cosmopolitan was garish in the best juke-box style of the time. The row of buttons is reminiscent of organ knobs. The instrument directly in front of the driver was the clock instead of the speedometer. Stylists had run amok. *Ford Motor Company*

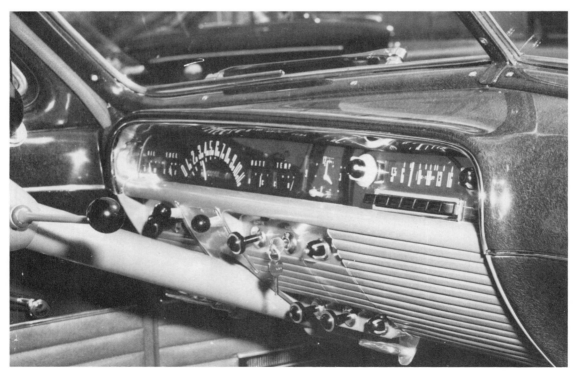

In 1950, the Lincoln and Cosmopolitan came out with a much improved instrument panel. This Lincoln version, virtually identical to the Cosmopolitan, places the speedometer directly in front of the driver. The control knobs are now given a better placement although the design stills seems a bit haphazard. *Lincoln-Mercury Division*

The 1951 Cosmopolitan instrument panel is about the same as 1950. The Hydramatic trans- mission control dial is now visible, offered first in June of 1950. *Ford Motor Company*

step plates under the rear fenders, red lights in the front bumpers, spotlights, flag holders and, in 1954, the famous bubble top. The car weighed 6,450 pounds and used the standard 152 bhp engine. It was replaced in 1961 but continued in use for the Ford Motor Company as a VIP car. It was used by President Lyndon Johnson in October 1965 in New York City and was finally placed in the Henry Ford Museum in 1967.

Identification

The 1949 Lincoln has the "frowning" grille with the ends turning sharply downward. The parking lights are circular. The instrument panel has two circular dials and the controls are a row of square buttons, nicely made and somewhat confusing to use. The windshield is two piece.

The 1949 Cosmopolitan has the big slab sides with a very heavy chrome trim strip over the front wheel arch. The windshield is one piece. All windows are outlined in stainless steel.

The 1950 grille for both cars is squared off with a single center bar. The parking lights are rectangular. The dashboard is redesigned with a semicircular speedometer set directly in front of the driver, the whole ensemble under an asymmetrical hood.

The 1951 grille has a center horizontal section with five vertical louvers. The heavy chrome strip over the Cosmopolitan front wheel arch is replaced by a full-length trim stripe. There are small fins, more noticeable on the Lincoln than the Cosmopolitan.

Serial numbers (engine numbers)

The 1949 Lincoln series are numbered 9EL1 to 9EL73,559.

The 1949 Cosmopolitan are numbered 9EH1 to 9EH73,563.

Note that the same sequence of numbers was used for both models. Engines numbers will exceed car production.

The 1950 Lincoln numbers are: 50LP5,001L to 50LP20,082L (LP = Lincoln Plant, Detroit), or 50LA5,001L to 50LA72,521L (LA = Los Angeles).

The 1950 Cosmopolitan numbers are: 50LP5,001H to 50LP15,701H (Cosmopolitans were built only in Detroit).

The 1951 Lincoln numbers are: 51LP (or LA) 5,001L, on up.

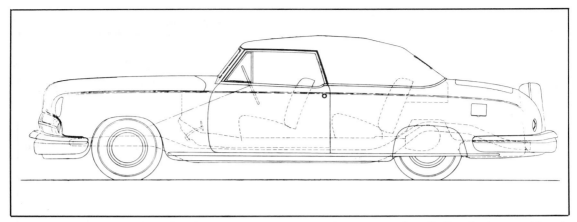

Robert Doehler prepared this Continental cabriolet design for the 1949 Cosmopolitan chassis. The drawing is dated July 9, 1946. The only echo of the original Continental is the angularity of the side window and the outside mounted spare. The roundness of Gregorie's Cosmopolitan does not work well. But the key problem is that the windshield is way too far forward and the proportion of the original Continental has been lost. The design was not produced. *Ford Motor Company*

The first full sized clay which hints at the grille design of the 1949 Lincoln. The date is November 17, 1941. There is a remarkable resemblance to the 1946 Oldsmobile. The 1949 Lincoln could well have been introduced in 1943, if the war had not intervened. *Ford Archives, Dearborn, Michigan*

This design was finished on June 26, 1945 and shows the notch-backed Cosmopolitan with what would be the 1949 Mercury grille. The pod trim over the front-wheel arch would be used in 1949 and on the rear in 1950. The slash accent stripes in modified form would appear in 1951. *Ford Archives, Dearborn, Michigan*

The 1951 Cosmopolitan numbers are: 51LP5,001H, on up.

Production

1949	Lincoln-all body styles	38,384
	H–72 Cosmopolitan 2–dr Club coupe	7,685
	H–73 Cosmopolitan Town sedan, fastback	7,302
	H–74 Cosmopolitan Sport sedan	18,906
	H–76 Cosmopolitan convertible	1,230
	Total	73,507
1950	L–72 & L72C Lincoln Club and Lido coupe	5,748
	L–74 Lincoln Sport sedan	11,741
	H–72 Cosmopolitan Club coupe	1,315
	H–72C Cosmopolitan Capri coupe	509
	H–74 Cosmopolitan Sport sedan	8,332
	H–76 Cosmopolitan convertible	536
	Total	28,181
1951	L–72B & L–72C Lincoln Club and Lido coupe	4,482

The interior of the White House No. 1 Cosmopolitan limousine had gold-plated fixtures, lizard-skin fitted cases in the arm rests, two thermos bottles and a radio control panel. The finish was unexcelled. *Ford Motor Company*

President Truman smiles broadly in the inaugural parade in January 1949 in a Cosmopolitan convertible. Two more Cosmopolitan convertibles followed plus two 16–cylinder Cadillacs and a Dodge convertible. Secret Service men rode in Jeepsters. Well to the rear behind the flag bearers is another row of Cosmopolitans flanked by Packard convertibles. Everyone was trying to get in the act but the President rode in a Lincoln. *Ford Motor Company*

L–74 Lincoln Sport sedan	12,279
H–72B Cosmopolitan Club coupe	1,476
H–72C Cosmopolitan Capri coupe	1,251
H–74 Cosmopolitan Sport sedan	12,229
H–76 Cosmopolitan convertible	857
Total	32,574

The Lincoln tradition of serving the White House continued with the ordering of ten 1949 limousines. They were assigned as follows:

9EHS 65387 President Truman; armor plated after assassination attempt on the president, November 1, 1950

9EHS68477 The president's wife, Bess Truman

9EHS68341 White House pool

9EHS68537 White House backup

9EHS69379 Secret Service (convertible)

Even before the great road cars of 1952–54, the Lincoln was doing well in competition. In this dramatic photo, Jesus Nava Gonzales manages to become airborne in his 1949 Lincoln. The event is the 1950 Carrera Panamericana, in which he finished 14th. *Ford Motor Company*

The well known "Bubble Top" Presidential Parade Car replaced the "Sunshine Special" in 1950 and served until 1961. The 145–inch wheelbase was used only on this car and the Presidential No. 1 limousine. *Ford Motor Company*

9EHS69120 Matthew L. Connelly, appointment secretary
9EHS69754 John Steelman, assistant to the president
9EHS69281 William Hassett, correspondence secretary
9EHS69380 White House pool

The tenth car was the Dietrich-built bubble top parade car.

In 1950, nine other limousines were built for government and Ford VIP use.

0LP6235–H Charles S. Murphy, special counsel
0LP6243–H State Department
0LP6239–H Ford Motor Company, New York City office
0LP6237–H Ford Motor Company, Metuchen, New Jersey
0LP6238–H Ford Motor Company, Metuchen, New Jersey
0LP6236–H Government of Israel
0LP6240–H Ford Motor Company, Chicago
0LP6241–H Ford Motor Company, San Francisco
0LP6241–H Ford Motor Company, Los Angeles

Problem areas

The 1949 cars were troubled by new model problems. The early engines had balancing problems, which were soon masked by redesigned motor mounts and later by revised balancing. Others matters which were corrected were camshaft scuffing, poor idling, noisy air cleaner, exhaust valve corrosion and sticking, and cylinder head cracking. Few engines that have survived forty years in service will suffer from these introduction problems but buyers may expect a certain roughness in the 1949 engines.

The bodies presented many early problems. The window winders broke glass, water leaks plagued the windshield and backlight, the door locks were sloppy, door lips were striking the body, and there were numerous rattles and noises. These problems were attacked vigorously and corrected, though an early 1949 Lincoln may feel "loose." Brakes grabbed and were modified. The frame thickness was increased from 0.104 to 0.119 inch to increase stiffness. Bigger shocks were specified.

The 1950 cars were much improved and had few mechanical problems. By 1951 the cars were even more refined, as is usually the case with continued production.

The Lincolns and Cosmopolitans were heavy and fast. Brake technology was simple and wear can be rapid. The same applies to shock absorbers which, on the new independent front suspension, had much work to do. Prudent buyers will look for weakness through a driving evaluation.

Market history

The early 1948 introduction of the 1949 Lincoln made for a booming market but when the competition unrolled the 1949 models in the fall of 1948, the glory days were over. By the following spring Lincoln sales were dropping. Though dealers grumbled, no relief appeared until January 27, 1950, when the 1950 models appeared. Thus the 1949 Lincoln was sold through twenty-one long months.

Especially important was the design of the 1948 Cadillac introduced three months before the 1949 Lincoln. This trendsetting design pioneered the tail fins. Furthermore, the Cadillac did not follow the slab-side styling of Hudson, Kaiser, Frazer, Nash and Packard. The rear fender was sculptured and would be further emphasized as new models appeared. Thus the Cosmopolitan dated very quickly with its Gregorie roundness. The 1950 Cadillac moved to a very square greenhouse which further made the Cosmopolitan and the Lincoln look out of date. Sales figures tell the story:

1949 model (21 months)—Lincoln 38,384; Cosmopolitan 35,123
1950 model (10 months)—Lincoln 17,489; Cosmopolitan 10,692
1951 model (13 months)—Lincoln 16,761; Cosmopolitan 15,813

On the used car market the Lincolns lost value quickly. In November 1954, the Kelley Blue Book suggested a retail price of $655 for a Cosmopolitan Sedan while a similar Cadillac 62, which cost $200 less when new, commanded $1,030. One year later the Lincoln market had virtually collapsed with retail values at $380. After 1952, the new image of Lincoln as a speed car with splendid

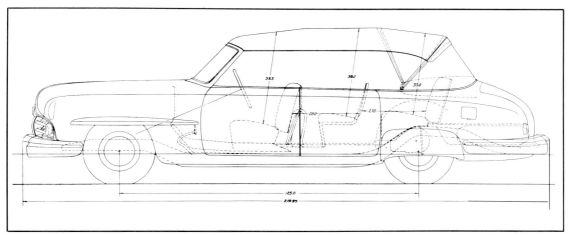

Here is a car which some collectors wish had been built. Martin Regitko drew this Custom Phaeton on May 7, 1948. It was designed on a 125–inch wheelbase. *Ford Archives, Dearborn, Michigan*

handling made the older cars seem all the more obsolete. Junking began in the mid-fifties and continued for a decade.

The beginning of collector interest came late. In the early seventies, the few remaining Cosmopolitans and the even rarer smaller Lincoln sedans could still be picked up for three figures. In 1977, top sedan values were no more than $2,000 with the convertibles between $4,500 and $5,000.

Interest picked up around 1980 and serious investor speculation got under way; by the end of 1982 the best Cosmopolitan convertibles were bringing $10,000, while the four-door sedans were around $3,000. The market slowly advanced in the eighties. At the end of 1987, top prices for the convertibles had moved to $16,000 with the sedans around $7,000. More likely was the sale of rather ordinary cars at one-half these prices

because the restoration costs still could not be justified.

At the end of 1989, convertible prices had worked their way up to perhaps $20,000 with the sedans at about $10,000, again for grade #1 cars.

Restorers have yet to make the big moves on these cars despite, or perhaps because of, their rarity. A condition #1 Cosmopolitan convertible made $30,500 at one of the Arizona sales in 1988. But only eight 1949–51 Lincolns appeared at auctions throughout the whole 1988 year which indicates how thin the market really is. The very scarcity of the cars has made them not only inaccessible to collectors but nearly invisible. There is no question that these splendid 1949–51 Lincolns will continue to gain in value during the nineties but only a select few will be able to savor their quality and charm.

Chapter 4

1952–54 Capri and Cosmopolitan

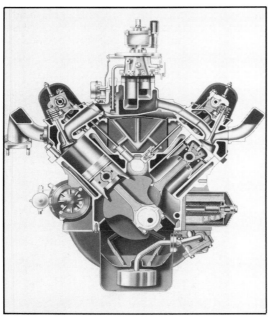

The new 1952 overhead-valve Lincoln engine displaced 317.5 cubic inches and produced 160 bph in its initial form, raised to 205 bph in 1953. The wedge shaped combustion chamber allowed big valves and good breathing. These engines were enormously strong; in the Pan American Race cars they were reliable at a sustained 5000 rpm for hour after hour. No other power plant of the period could match them, including even the foreign exotics. *Lincoln-Mercury Division*

History

The development of the 1952 Lincoln was the first positive result of the new organization team. Chief Engineer Earle S. MacPherson had the resources to build anything and he quickly stamped his technical expertise on the new car; in particular he introduced a splendid ball joint front suspension which revolutionized handling.

A fine new oversquare OHV engine with a 3.8–inch bore by 3.5–inch stroke had a capacity of 317.5 ci, down from the 1951 flathead's 337 ci. But brake horsepower was up to 160 at 3900 rpm. A wedge-shaped combustion chamber was not only new but offered excellent development prospects. The dual-range Hydra-matic was now standard with a 3.31:1 axle ratio. The wheelbase of the new car was 123 inches, midway between the 1951 Lincoln and Cosmopolitan. Tires were 8.00x15 but for convertibles were 8.20x15.

George Walker was now in charge of styling and the Ford products for 1952 had a common theme, namely a new angularity in the greenhouse with aggressive frontal appearance and smooth tapering to the rear. The specific Lincoln styling was handled by William Schmidt and Don DeLaRossa and featured a high-set front bumper which functioned as a centerpiece for the grille. It was a novel and clean idea which was widely copied, especially by Pontiac and Oldsmobile in 1955. The headlamps were set high and

Here is the factory photo of the 1952 Capri convertible, a balanced compact design which projects aggressive power. The superb style was matched by a brilliant engine and new front suspension. Only 1,191 convertibles were built in 1952, the lowest number of the 1952–54 series, and they are much coveted by collectors. *Ford Motor Company*

very forward in sharp contrast to the 1949–51 cars.

The Cosmopolitan name was now used for the standard line and Capri was the name chosen for the deluxe editions. The club coupe was a proper pillarless hardtop in both series.

It was apparent that these new Lincolns had great road potential; 100 mph speed was matched by superb handling. On the negative side was tire technology which was not up to sustained high-speed use.

For 1953, horsepower was raised to 205 at 4200 rpm and torque was up to 305 lb-ft over the range of 2300 to 3000 rpm. This was all that was needed to make the Lincoln a world beater and it finished 1–2–3–4 in the 1952 Pan American Road Race on November 20. The late date allowed the 1953 model to be used. The winning cars were highly tuned, the engines producing close to 300 bhp. Meticulous preparation by Bill Stroppe and Clay Smith was the secret of victory, with special attention to the suspension. These cars were capable of 130 mph. The penalty was tire wear; the three team cars used 100 tires.

Styling changes were minor and unnecessary in 1953 as sales soared. Power options

The 1952 ball joint suspension was all new and was a key ingredient in making the Lincolns safe at 130 mph in the Pan American Road races. The elimination of the traditional king pin has simplified the structure and brought more direct control of the road wheels. The ball joints must be kept well lubricated for they bear heavy loads. *Lincoln-Mercury Division*

The basic four-door 1952 Cosmopolitan sedan was a neat package even without white wall tires. The high headlamp placement and forward leaning rear door slash stripe gave an aggressive appearance. These sedans have not survived in any numbers as collectors usually sought more sporting body styles. *Ford Motor Company*

were emphasized for 1953 including four-way power seats, power steering, vacuum power brakes and power window lifts.

The changes for 1954 were in response to some criticism that the Lincoln was now too compact when compared with the luxury competition. Much chrome trim was added and the car looked heavier and also longer. Brake lining size went up from 202 to 220 square inches, a useful improvement in light of the Lincoln's high speeds. Sales success continued, and the car was steadily refined. The stock 1954 car could accelerate from zero to sixty in 12.4 seconds. Gasoline mileage was about 12 mpg.

Success in the Pan American Road Race continued also with a 1–2–3–4 finish in 1953 and a 1–2 finish (in private hands) in November 1954. These great cars could hold 130 mph on a 3.07:1 axle with the engine turning at 5000 rpm. With Stroppe's careful preparation, they were dead reliable and unbeatable. A stock 1954 Lincoln could reach 115 mph. However, Clay Smith was killed at a track in Illinois on September 6, 1954, which deprived the winning team of his skills.

Identification

The 1952 Lincolns, compact and aggressive, are recognized by the high-set bumper/grille, the projecting headlamps and the diagonal slash stripe delineating the rear fenders. The model name, Cosmopolitan or Capri, is on the rear fender.

The 1953 Lincolns have the block "Lincoln" at the base of the hood above the grille.

The popular 1952 Cosmopolitan Sport Coupe was offered for $3293 at the factory. The accessory list was growing and could add hundreds to the base price. This model, and the uptrimmed Capri version, are much sought after by collectors. Marc Hennig owns this fine example. *Tim Howley*

The Lincoln medallion is removed from the hood and a "V" insignia appears in the center of the grille. The model name continues on the rear fender.

The 1954 Lincolns have the "V" on the front of the hood with a center medallion. The diagonal slash stripe is gone from the rear fender and a second lower trim stripe is set just above the wheel arch. The model name is on the rear fender.

Serial numbers

1952 Cosmopolitan—52LP5,001 to 52WA29,217H (LP = Lincoln Plant, WA = Wayne, the new Lincoln assembly plant). 1952 Capri—52LA5,4001H to 52LA7,761H; also 52SL5,001H to 52SL5,072H (LA = Los Angeles, SL = St. Louis).
1953 Cosmopolitan and Capri—53WA5001H to 53WA39,566H; also 53LA5,001H to 53LA10,995H.

The 1952 instrument panel had white on black legibility, positive heating controls and a generally functional layout. The legible speedometer was, if anything, limited with a top reading of 110 mph. A stock Lincoln could do 100 on the level and given a little downhill run combined with the usual speedometer optimism, the needle could be pinned. *Ford Motor Company*

This 1953 Lincoln Cosmopolitan sedan is little changed from the 1952 model. The big news for 1953 was the full power offerings in braking, steering, and four way seat adjustment. The V insignia on the rear fender commemorates the golden anniversary of the Ford Motor Company. Though 7,560 Cosmopolitans sedans were built in 1953, few have survived. *Ford Motor Company*

This splendid 1953 Capri hardtop was the subject of a $130,000 restoration and may well be the finest example extant. With the 205 bhp engine, it is a fine performer and represents the best of Lincoln design of the period. It is owned by Henry Wheeler. *L.C.O.C.*

1954 Cosmopolitan and Capri—
54WA5,001H to 54WA36,840H; also
54LA5,001H to 54LA9,981H.

Production

1952	60A Capri coupe	5,681
	76A Capri convertible	1,191
	60C Cosmopolitan Sport coupe	4,545
	73A Cosmopolitan 4–dr sedan	
	73B Capri 4–dr sedan	15,854
	Total	27,271
1953	60C Cosmopolitan hardtop coupe	6,562
	73A Cosmopolitan sedan	7,560
	60A Capri hardtop coupe	12,916
	73B Capri sedan	11,352
	76A Capri convertible	2,372
	Total	40,762
1954	60C Cosmopolitan hardtop coupe	2,904
	73A Cosmopolitan sedan	4,447
	60A Capri hardtop coupe	14,003

The 1953 Capri convertible is a target car for many collectors. Simple block letters on the front of the hood replaced the 1952 insignia. The protruding bumper guards on the front represent the stylist's attempt to lengthen the car to match the luxury competition. The compact idea was great but Lincoln would inevitably grow and, in the process, lose the performance image. This car is owned by Ed Poole. *Tim Howley*

Here is the rugged chassis of the 1953 Lincoln as used for the hardtop and convertible. An extra cross member ties the center of the X-member to the side rails. This fine strong chassis can be weakened by years of corrosion. Buyers of weathered cars should check the frame members. *Ford Motor Company*

73B Capri sedan	13,598
76A Capri convertible	1,951
Total	36,903

Problem areas

The 1952–54 cars were engineers' cars and had an enviable reliability record. Routine maintenance and lubrication was assumed and neglect over the years may mean worn ball joints and a degrading of the fine handling. Check the Hydra-matic transmission for leaks. Be more concerned about slipping than about hard or jerking shifts which indicate that the Hydra-matic is working smartly.

The side trim was changed for 1954 and the angle heavy slash stripe was removed. Strong horizontal brightwork was an effort by the stylists to lengthen the car. Compare this rear bumper with that of the 1952, another effort by the stylists to add length. Ruth Boruck owns this excellent example. The driving pleasure and refinement were never higher. *Tim Howley*

The engines were strong and gave high mileage with few troubles. Mechanical repair parts are now obtainable and good club support has helped keep these great cars on the road. Be especially careful when confronting cars with deteriorated body and trim parts, items which are now scarce.

Market history

The public acceptance of the 1952–54 Lincoln was strong. In the used car marketplace, when measuring percentage of retained value against new car prices, Lincoln pulled ahead of Chrysler for the first time. At the end of 1954, a 1952 Lincoln Capri sedan retained 56 percent of its value; a 1952 Chrysler Saratoga 8 sedan, slightly cheaper when new, retained 43 percent of its value; the 1952 Packard 300 Sedan, again slightly cheaper than the Lincoln, retained 48 per-

The 1954 Capri convertible was the final statement of the 1952 design, still very compact, neat and beautifully balanced. Collectors love to find these cars but the market remains thin. Only 1,951 were built and most have been lost. *Ford Motor Company*

This factory photo of the 1954 Capri sedan in black emphasizes the very strong chrome trim used. The width of the trim emphasizes weight, perhaps a deliberate attempt of the stylists to create the illusion of bulk in order to meet the competition. Lincoln would soon grow. *Ford Motor Company*

cent of its value; and the Cadillac 62 sedan, more expensive than the Lincoln, retained 72 percent of its value. The Lincoln was gaining.

The utility of the 1952–54 cars continued well into the sixties; then prices slowly sank to junking levels. Enthusiasts and nostalgic owners, however, retained a fondness for the series and many more survived into the seventies when true collecting began. By the end of the seventies, the prices for excellent sedans were still below $2,000. Even good convertibles were in the $4,500 range, lower than the 1949–51 series. The 1954 model was seen as slightly more valuable than the 1953 with the 1952 bringing up the rear.

By the fall of 1982, prices were rising strongly. Superb condition #1 convertibles were nearing $10,000 with the hardtops at around $5,000. There were still many sec- ond- and third-level cars available at very low prices. Appreciation continued in the eighties and was stronger as the "muscle car" phenomenon took hold among collec- tors. The 1952–54 Lincolns were correctly seen as the first great road cars, and by the fall of 1987, prices had caught up with the 1949–51 cars. Convertibles were now at $15,000 or higher with the hardtops around $9,000. By 1989 the convertibles had moved into the $25,000 range with the hardtops at about half that price. Attention seemed to focus on the 1953 model which has the big horsepower engine, the slightly smaller and lighter body, and the many power options.

Auction entries for 1988 were very thin and only six examples appeared on the cir- cuit. But there is a larger survival rate of these cars than for the earlier models and the market is more active.

There seems every likelihood that this splendid Lincoln will continue to appreciate strongly into the nineties.

★★★★★	**Convertibles**
★★★★	**Hardtops**
★★★	**All others**

1955–57 Custom, Capri and Premiere

History

The 1955 Lincoln continued to use the well-proven body dies of the 1952–54 series and the stylists succeeded in producing an unusually clean revision. The grille was simplified with fine horizontal bars. The chrome trimming was slightly muted and the effect was simple and uncluttered.

The great V–8 engine was bored out fourteen-thousandths to 341 ci and horse-power was raised to 225 with a 8.5:1 conversion ratio. The Hydra-matic was replaced by a new three-speed Turbo Drive which mated with a 3.07:1 rear axle. This low axle ratio was chosen to help offset poor gasoline mileage. Smooth high-speed cruising was the Lincon's strong point and there was no better handling car on the road.

Air conditioning was spreading throughout the industry and Lincoln offered a brand new system in 1955 which was combined

The original 1952 shell was given a major modification for 1955. Length was added in the rear fender blades. The angular slash stripe returned ahead of the rear wheels. In a time of growing bizarre styling, the Lincoln was unusually clean.

Horsepower was now 225. Discerning collectors find in this transition model the final statement of the great Lincoln road cars. It was a handsome automobile. *Ford Motor Company*

with a 3.31 axle ratio. The array of power accessories continued.

For 1955 only, the Cosmopolitan name was replaced by the "Custom" while the Capri continued as the top-of-the-line model.

This superb car should have been a smash hit but it was caught in a marketing squeeze. The 1955 Cadillac was mounted on a 129–inch wheelbase and the new Chrysler Imperial was on a 128–inch wheelbase. Both looked bigger than the Lincoln and since luxury was perceived as size, the Lincoln's compact virtues seemed out of date. Lincoln's management listened and ordered development of the 1958 model which would outsize them all. It seemed like a prudent decision.

For 1956, the top-of-the-line model was called the Premiere and the Capri replaced the Custom. The Lincoln wheelbase was extended to 126 inches on which was set a beautiful new design of unusual simplicity. From the hooded headlamps to the extended rear fender blades, there was a long un-broken line with a low chrome spear extend-ing from the front wheel arch to the rear. The Industrial Designers Institute gave its award to Lincoln Premiere hardtop on June 21.

Also for 1956, engine displacement moved up to 368 ci, with 285 bhp and 401 lb-ft of

Optional plexiglass roofs first appeared in 1954 but they were a short lived novelty. Solar heat was substantial despite tinting and the plexi-glass was easily scratched. The advertising theme for this 1955 Lincoln Premiere was "See the gay lights of theater row." Good examples of the plexiglass roof are very rare and much coveted. *Ford Motor Company*

torque on a 9:1 compression ratio. Top speed was around 105 mph. Gasoline mileage would be about 11 mpg, about the same as 1955. Twelve-volt electrics appeared just in time to crank the big new engine and supply power to myriad electric devices. Colors, fabrics and leather were richer than ever before.

With an early introduction on September 25, 1955, the 1956 car had a record setting sales year.

The face lift for 1957 yielded to the tail fin craze; the rear blades were extended to very sharp points and a slash stripe appeared on the side panel to mark the beginning of the rear fender line. The beautiful smoothness

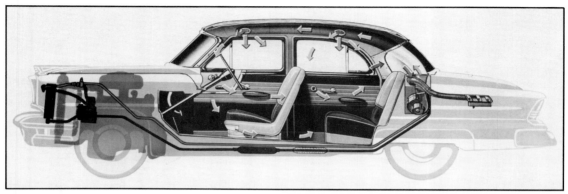

The new Lincoln air-conditioning system for 1955 used transparent tubes behind the rear seats to conduct air to ceiling outlets. It was a nice idea but there was no air directly ahead of the front seat where it was really needed. This design was replaced in 1958 by a forward mounted system. These units can still do the job but there is a lot of plumbing to look after. *Ford Motor Company*

This 1956 Lincoln Premiere four door in a dark finish sets off the new body design highlights. A longer wheelbase of 126 inches gave more freedom for the stylists. Gone were the slash stripes and the hints of a rear fender as one unbroken body crease emphasized the greater length. Tom Snortum is the owner of this award winning car. *L.C.O.C.*

The Industrial Designers Institute gave its award to this Premiere model on June 21, 1956. Engine displacement was up to 368 ci producing 285 bhp and 401 pounds feet of torque. Twelve-volt electrics arrived just in time to meet growing power needs. Sales for the 1956 model year set a record of 50,322. Collectors have always liked this beautiful car and values are strong. *Ford Motor Company*

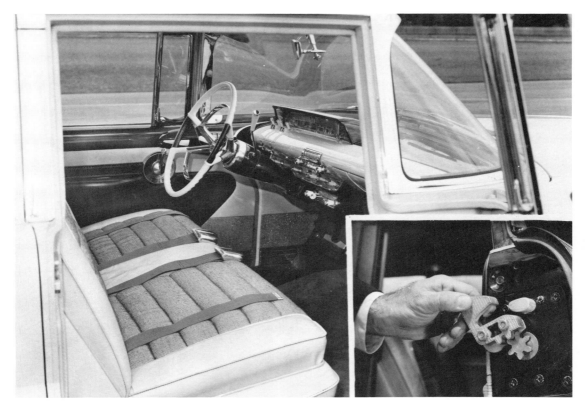

Refinement touches in 1956 included the rotary door locks, pioneered by Chrysler in 1940. The pleats were now horizontal and five fabrics were offered plus leather. There were twenty-nine colors available. Seatbelts were also a novelty. *Ford Motor Company*

of 1956 was gone. Stylist David Ash introduced quad lamps which were mounted one above the other. The car was "glitzier" and restrained only when compared to its rivals.

The 368–inch engine was tuned to 300 bhp on a higher 10:1 compression and torque moved up to 415 lb-ft. Performance and handling remained strong.

Sales were down some 18 percent from 1956 but the market was very competitive.

Identification

The following styling treatments can quickly identify the year:

The 1955 Lincoln had fine horizontal bars behind the massive high-set bumper. "Lincoln" was in block letters on the hood above the grille.

The 1956 Lincoln had hooded headlamps, no belt line chrome but a long chrome spear at the rocker panels. Long parking lamps were set in the bumper. The A-pillar was vertical with a wraparound windshield.

The 1957 Lincoln had very pointed rear fins with a diagonal slash strip delineating the rear fender area. Quad headlamps were set vertically.

Serial numbers

Serial numbers and engine totals may be intermixed. The numbers below for 1955 Wayne and Los Angeles production exceed listed Custom and Capri production by 890 units. It should be noted that the Mark II used the same block and perhaps some production may have been allocated which could affect totals, even with different serial numbers. Also note that the 1956 and 1957 number totals have no relationship to production. The serial number's utility lies in the opening codes, i.e. the year and place of manufacture (55WA—or 56LA—). The total numbers for three years exceed production figures by 968 units.

1955—55WA5,001H to 55WA28,595H (Wayne, Michigan); also 55LA5,001H to 55LA8,519H (Los Angeles).

1956—56WA5,001L to 56WA48,056L (approximate); also 56LA5,001L to 56LA12,288L.

1957—57WA5,001L to 57WA46,232L.

Production

1955	60C Custom 2–dr hardtop	1,362
	73A Custom 4–dr sedan	2,187
	60A Capri 2–dr hardtop	11,462
	73B Capri 4–dr sedan	10,724
	76A Capri convertible	1,487
	Total	27,222
1956	60E Capri 2–dr hardtop	4,355

The interior of the 1956 Premiere convertible was flashy. The bench seats were in luxurious leather. Some 2,447 lucky new buyers enjoyed this car and collectors today prize this model. Prices are strong and climbing. *Lincoln-Mercury Division*

A German hearse body mounted on the 1956 chassis. The way to go! *Gene Babow*

	73A Capri 4–dr sedan	4,436
	60B Premiere 2–dr hardtop	19,619
	73B Premiere 4–dr sedan	19,465
	76B Premiere convertible	2,447
	Total	50,322
1957	57A Capri 4–dr landau	
	hardtop sedan	1,451
	58A Capri 4–dr sedan	1,476
	60A Capri 2–dr hardtop	2,973
	57B Premiere 4–dr landau	
	hardtop sedan	11,223
	58B Premiere 4–dr sedan	5,139
	60B Premiere 2–dr hardtop	15,185
	75B Premiere convertible	3,676
	Total	41,123

Problem areas

A peculiar problem involves the 1956 taillights. The exhaust was routed through the bumper and required a sharp turn which often burned out at the elbow. Exhaust gases then went straight into the taillight assembly and often melted the lens. The 1956 taillight replacements are extremely expensive.

Transmission trouble is indicated by several symptoms. Club member Gary Schwertley points out that slipping is a danger signal, as are leaks. Front leaks are usually caused by a bad front pump seal. A rare source of transmission leaks is the speedometer cable fitting. A more uncommon symptom is noise or banging which could be a bad flex plate which transmits power to the torque converter. The steel flanges on the plate may break. In the 1957 transmission, similar "ears" may fatigue and break.

Power steering units may leak through the Pitman arm and a seal kit for the Saginaw unit is available as also used on the Cadillac. Fortunately, parts are available to rebuild transmissions, power steering units and engines, and they are surprisingly reasonable.

Market history

The years of 1955 to 1957 were golden years for Lincoln, and the public embraced the car. Used car retained value is a measurement of a car's acceptance which is an important test used by management.

Using September 1963 as a convenient measurement point, the seven-year-old 1956 Lincoln was approaching low levels but the fine Premiere hardtop could still command $615 retail in the Kelley Blue Book. Collectors were not yet interested. The Premiere convertible was only $495. For the first time

This 1957 Capri uses the 1956 sheet metal but new and lethal tailfins have been added. Fins were endemic in those days and Lincoln's version is more restrained than others. Very few Capri sedans were built; buyers usually bought the upscale Premiere. Survivors are rare. *Ford Motor Company*

The 1957 Premiere convertible is a choice car for collectors and values for it, along with all other open cars of the period, are climbing rapidly. *Tim Howley*

The Premiere two-door hard top was the most popular Lincoln for 1957 and 15,185 were sold. The quad headlamps are really two fog lamps mounted beneath the regular lights. The tailfins really dominate the design. Pity the pedestrian who might become impaled! *Ford Motor Company*

Cadillacs were not a runaway in used car values. The 1956 Cadillacs were rated at $740 and the Imperial was at $645.

The 1957 models were still active in the used market and the Lincoln Premiere hardtop made $835, 16 percent of the new base price. The comparable Cadillac DeVille at the same new base price was retailing at $1,160, 23 percent of new cost. The Imperial Crown two-door was $1,085, 20 percent of the original price.

By the middle of the sixties all of these cars were being junked. Collector interest began slowly and, as always, was marked by the appreciation of the convertible above the closed cars, in contrast to normal used car depreciation. By the late seventies, the 1955 and 1956 convertibles were reaching $5,000 with the 1957 convertible trailing at about $4,000. The closed cars were bringing about $2,000. It should be remembered that many original but worn closed cars could still be bought for under $1,000 in the seventies.

The turning point was in the eighties, when values climbed quickly. By 1982, the convertibles were around $9,000; collectors had made their choice and the 1956 convertible was bringing a premium. The 1955 Capri hardtop was popular at around $5,000 trailed by the 1955 Premiere at $4,000 and the 1957 Premiere at $3,800.

This pattern of relative value shifted slightly through the mid-eighties. In June 1986, convertibles for 1956 had reached $17,000; the 1955, $12,500; and the 1957, $14,500. For hardtops the 1956 Premiere was the clear champion at $9,000, the 1955 Capri was $6,700 and the 1957 Premiere was $6,500.

The Lincoln market boiled upward as collectors recognized the superb qualities of these cars. But in addition to quality, collectors seemed to prefer size and drama, and by mid-1989 the 1957 Premiere convertible achieved top value at $28,000, followed by the 1956 and 1955 models. The hardtop market was around $12,000. Thus in three years, Lincoln prices doubled, in the estimate of *Old Cars Price Guide*. Other estimators of the market were not quite as optimistic and saw top values for convertibles around $20,000. Again auction results are minimal and usually deal with average condition cars. Condition #3 convertibles could still be purchased for $10,000 with closed cars in the low four figures.

For the nineties the market will continue to advance for these very desirable cars. The annual rate of appreciation through the eighties for the 1955–57 cars has been approximately 20 percent per year. If this rate continues, and using a $20,000 base figure for 1989, a Lincoln convertible will be worth about $150,000 in the year 2000.

Chapter 6

1955–57 Continental Mark II

History

John R. Davis headed a new committee formed on January 29, 1951, to consider product expansion. Davis and his senior advisors concluded that another Continental was needed for several reasons. If Lincoln were to recapture the top of the luxury market, it needed a prestige leader for image rebuilding.

The 1952–1954 Lincoln had been targeted to compete with the Oldsmobile by Harold Youngren. The Oldsmobile 88 had been a performance leader when introduced in 1949 and the Lincoln not only was about the same size but had eclipsed the Oldsmobile as a performance leader. But in the process the luxury market was abandoned. Lincoln no longer offered a limousine and the four-door sedan was too compact for formal use. Even if a car were to be designed especially for the luxury market, Lincoln did not have the production facilities to go head to head against Cadillac. But the forthcoming success of Cadillac Eldorado at $7,465, twice the price of the Cadillac 62, suggested an untapped market at prices hitherto considered unrealistic; Lincoln took notice.

There was also a nostalgic feeling about the 1940–1948 Continental which had never faded among Lincoln corporate leaders.

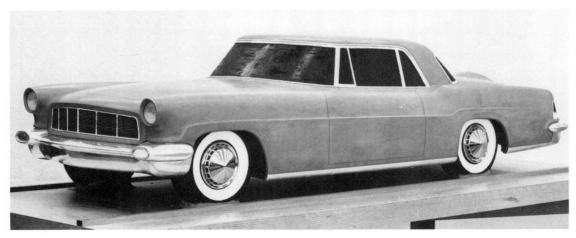

A clay model of the Continental Mark II appeared in the late spring of 1953. Apart from the hubcaps, the grille, and bumper guards, the design is final. *Ford Motor Company*

The handsome formality of the Mark II is enhanced by a formal pose in front of Denison University. The very long hood sets the small greenhouse well back on the chassis which recalls the classic look of the original Continental. Designer John Reinhart's extraordinary restraint is very evident and must be appreciated in the light of the excesses of the period. It was a very great achievement. *Ford Motor Company*

A 1956 Mark II, owned by Robb De Mille Petty, stands by a 1937 Lincoln Zephyr. Many of these Mark IIs have been maintained in near perfect condition. The quality of the car is evident everywhere, a source of satisfaction to loving owners. The Mark II is one of those very rare cars which have been seen as a classic from the moment they were first produced. *Tim Howley*

This convertible was prepared for Mrs. William Clay Ford by Derham and has the serial number C56G3190. It is the only factory authorized convertible. It is now owned by Walter Goeppinger. *L.C.O.C.*

When it became apparent that the forthcoming 1949 Lincoln and Cosmopolitan spelled the end of the original Continental, Lincoln stylist Robert Doehler was asked to make studies for a replacement; Doehler soon realized that it was impossible to graft a "Continental look" on the 1949 cars and the project was abandoned.

The urge for a new Continental continued to be so strong that on July 1, 1952, a Separate Products Division was formed under William Clay Ford. The purpose of this division was to design a new Continental outside of the normal constraints of Lincoln styling.

Ford called in Harley Copp, Gordon Buehrig and John Reinhart. Reinhart was put in charge of styling and was directed to produce a series of evolutionary designs starting with the last 1948 Continental. These were rejected by Henry Ford II in late 1952.

A second try was made and, in addition, four outside consulting designers were invited to prepare sketches. On April 2, 1953, thirteen unsigned proposals were independently evaluated by each member of the Executive Committee. Reinhart's second design won and a full-size clay was ready on June 25. From that moment on, the development proceeded rapidly.

The new Continental was a quality-without-compromise job. Every decision about paint, cloth, leather, hardware and engineering was a search for the best. Running gear was standard Lincoln with rigorous additional testing and balancing. Body panels were fitted and then disassembled for simul-

Other convertibles have been produced from the Mark II body. Here is C56H3206 owned by Jack Bowser. *Tim Howley*

taneous painting to ensure perfect color match. Triple plating was standard practice. There was the consciousness among all employees that this was to be the "perfect" car.

Introduction was in October 1955 at Paris, Dearborn and major US cities with William Clay Ford personally greeting selected guests. The price was $10,000 but even at that exceptionally high level, fall sales were sensational and 1,251 units were built in 1955. Demand slackened dramatically in early 1956 and total production for the year was 1,307. In the opening months of 1957, only 442 cars were built. Production ceased on May 8, 1957. At $10,000 the car was very expensive. Even at that, Ford lost $1,000 on each car.

Identification

The buyer should be alert to the enthusiasm with which Lincoln enthusiasts approach the Continental Mark II. It is a pinnacle and target car for many and great attention has been focused on it. A good clean car can certainly be bought without great difficulty since so many are well cared for. But if one is headed for perfection, as many Mark II owners seem to be, the path is complex. The finest details do not escape the eye of the enthusiast.

To settle disputes about restoration and identification, the L.C.O.C. has published a forty-eight-page Authenticity Manual edited by Robert J. Prins with the help of twelve experts. It is a fine example of the dedication of members of the L.C.O.C. and it is a useful aid for serious collectors.

The Mark II's large grille contained fine squares set behind five vertical bars. The trunk lid had the distinctive Continental spare bulge. All standard cars were two-door hardtops. Derham built one convertible, C56G3190, for Mrs. William Clay Ford which was announced on October 12, 1956. It has been owned for many years by L.C.O.C. member Walter Goeppinger. A second convertible, C56E2997, body number 01-1E6L-328-1, was customized in Palm Beach without factory authority.

Serial numbers

The Continental Mark II identification code, C56, is followed by a month build code as follows:

The 1956 Model

Built in 1955: 6 = June, 7 = July, 8 = Aug. 9 = Sept., 0 = Oct., A = Nov., B = Dec. Built in 1956: C = Jan., D = Feb., E = March, F = Apr. G = May, H = June, I = July, J = Aug.

The 1957 Model

Built in 1956: K = Sept., L = Oct., M = Nov., N = Dec. Built in 1957: P = Jan., Q = Feb., R = March, S = Apr. T = May. (end production)

The first production Continental was C56 6975. C56 6977 was completed on June 24, 1955. The last was C56 T3989.

The 1956s ended on September 30, 1956. The 1957s reputedly begin with K3414 or K3418 according to club member Bob Davis, but note that these are November production numbers.

Colors

Many colors were offered. The following body codes appear as the first two digits of the body specification number on the patent plate:

01 = Black
02 = Cobalt blue iridescent
04 = Pastoral blue
05 = Forest green iridescent
07 = Naiad green
08 = Briar brown iridescent
10 = Sandalwood
11 = Dark grey iridescent
13 = Dark red
14 = Starmist white
15 = Medium blue
16 = Medium green (1956 only)
17 = Medium beige (1956 only)
18 = Medium grey (1956 only)
19 = Lucite medium blue iridescent (1957 only)
20 = Lucite medium green iridescent (1957 only)
21 = Lucite medium tan iridescent (1957 only)
22 = Lucite medium grey iridescent (1957 only)
885 = White lucite

There were five tu-tone combinations (upper/lower):
02 = Cobalt blue iridescentl/15 = Medium blue
05 = Forest green iridescent/16 = Medium green
08 = Briar brown iridescent/17 = Medium beige
11 = Dark grey iridescent/18 = Medium grey
11 = Deep grey/14 = Starmist white

Production

Production according to Ford Motor Company is as follows:
1955—1,251
1956—1,307
1957— 442
Total—3,000

Note that this summary does not agree with the serial numbers beginning with 975 and ending with 3989, which would total 3,015 cars. Debate continues on this matter.

Distinguished owners include the following:

John Daly (3408), Les Brown (2337), Walter Brennan (2350), Cecil B DeMille (2425), Harvey Firestone, Jr. (2894), Benson Ford (1281), Benson Ford (3278), Henry Ford II (1762), Ernest Kanzler (2028), Barry Goldwater (2408), Bill Harrah (2054), Stewart Granger (1806), Spike Jones (3608), Rogers Hornsby (2369), Henry J. Kaiser (1927), Henry J. Kaiser (2977), Louis Prima (3668), President Sukarno (3341), R.J. Reynolds (1988), Shah of Iran (2135), Frank Sinatra (1884), Igor Sikorsky (1918), Michael Todd (3978), Jack Warner (2815), Nelson Rockefeller (1568), Andrew Wyeth (1765), Daryl Zanuck (2737), William E Hutton (2254).

Problem areas

The Continental Mark II was the most carefully constructed automobile of its time and no effort was spared to achieve perfection. Engineering was up to date and components were proven and reliable. Yet two factors worked against the car.

The first was weight. A passenger-laden Continental easily exceeded 5,500 pounds and the brakes had a lot of work to do. Wear was rapid and fade was common. The second was complexity. Designers spared nothing for a perfection of luxury which meant adding an unusual (for the time) number of electric motors, switches, relays, solenoids, bulbs and the necessary wiring. Time inevitably degraded performance and problems are possible.

Among minor ills are the following items:

• The engine may run rough and stall. Check for a vacuum leak at the compensating valve which may be caused by the brake pedal depressing too far.

• Transmissions may leak after prolonged storage and may sometimes be cured with proprietary transmission seal fluid. Check for front spring sag.

• Power steering leaks occur, usually at the control valve on the pump cover or at the sector shaft oil seal.

Market history

The extraordinary reception of the Mark II in October of 1955 was short lived. The $10,000 price tag was daunting, two and one half times the price of the Lincoln and the Cadillac 62. Even the Cadillac Eldorado convertible seemed cheap at $6,286.

The market faltered in January 1956, only three months after the introduction, and discounting began, fatal to the image of the car. Every effort was made to improve the situation including direct mail to 50,000 people with high net worth and a reduction of the dealer force to sharpen sales methods. As the 1957 models appeared, unchanged, it was obvious that the game was over.

The fault with the original Mark II marketing by Ford in 1955 was a failure to identify the target buyer. The 1940 Continental had a medium price, extraordinary styling and the sense of being a personal car. The 1955 Mark II had a high price, good styling and was too large to be personal. The Ford Thunderbird would soon meet the 1940 categories more precisely than the Mark II.

Five years later, the 1956 Mark II had a retail value of $2,500, 25 percent of new cost. The Cadillac Eldorado could make only $1,110, barely 17 percent of its new cost. The 1957 Mark II would bring $2,935, 29 percent of new cost, while the Eldorado commanded $1,685, 23 percent of new price. Inasmuch as the 1957 Mark II was probably sold with some discount, it is clear that the Continental was doing very well.

The Mark II escaped junking. Many were neglected and stored but resale values never reached the point where people simply abandoned the cars. Through it all, the magic of the name and the sense that this car was something special remained to sustain value. Thus the Mark II has always been a collectible. Values rarely fell below $2,000 in the early sixties and prices were around $3,000 in 1966. Genuine appreciation was under way by 1970 with prices climbing to the $5,000 region. By 1978, the Mark II in flawless condition could command up to $14,000—three times the price of comparable Lincolns and Eldorados.

Interest in the Mark II was steady but the market remained relatively flat in the early eighties as other cars caught up. In 1986, the Mark II easily passed $20,000 and in three more years would touch $30,000. By this time, however, it was no longer a standout collectible and even the gargantuan 1960 Mark V was drawing close in value.

The reason for this leveling off is not hard to explain: They are not rare. Almost all of the Mark IIs are extant, creating a relatively large pool of cars that appear frequently in auctions. In a good auction in 1988, a beautiful Mark II could reach $40,000 or more, yet in provincial sales the same condition car might bring only $20,000. Faced with such an uncertain market and a large number of sales, the market does not move quickly.

Furthermore, collecting tastes have changed. In the early seventies, the Mark II was seen as a standout collectible which accounts for its early high value. This may reflect the original claims and purposes of the Ford company which were simply to build a "super car" of conspicuous elegance. The Mark II is a very good car indeed but those claims from the fall of 1955 now seem naive in light of the growing sophistication of collectors worldwide. As is the case with almost all collectible cars, demand begins when a mature and wealthy person looks back to a youthful golden age of dreaming and coveting and buys what could not be afforded long ago. Young people in 1955 did not see the Mark II as a target car because it did not represent youthful aspirations of speed, litheness and sex appeal. These subtle emotions may yet influence current collecting patterns.

The Mark II should continue to appreciate in a steady way in the nineties. Buyers should be aware of the broad market and the opportunity to find a very good example at a fair price. The superb quality of these cars will keep them on the road for a long time to come.

John Reinhart attempted to design a Continental Mark III combining John Najjar's new 1958 Lincoln with the themes of the Mark II. The huge size of the 1958 car was emphasized by the rear fins and the end result had little relationship with the Mark II. The project was soon abandoned. *Ford Motor Company*

Chapter 7

1958–60 Lincoln Capri and Premiere, 1958 Lincoln Continental Mark III, 1959 Mark IV and 1960 Mark V

History

The new chief stylist, John Najjar, set to work in 1955 on the 1958 Lincoln. Both sales and management executives were conscious of the Lincoln's limited size, and Najjar was told by Earle MacPherson to provide more interior room than Cadillac. In the search for "fresh individuality," Najjar sought to avoid both the Cadillac fin and the Chrysler wedge by using strong angularity. The rear fender blades were canted outward and were matched by the front headlamps, set vertically, giving the front a curious appearance dubbed the "Chinese look" by critics. There was concave sculpturing on the side of the car, including a novel concave space behind the front wheel arch. The design was strong and different.

The car had a longer wheelbase of 131 inches but the real novelty was the total

The 1958 Continental Mark III two door was a gigantic automobile. Stylist John Najjar was ordered to design a car with larger interior dimensions than Cadillac. Big dimensions combined with outward angled rear fender blades and headlamps resulted in an enormous vehicle. The unit body construction was the largest ever attempted and development problems were great. Few of these cars have survived. *L.C.O.C.*

length of the car, 229 inches, a record for the industry. Weight was around 4,800 pounds. The truly remarkable thing about all of this size and weight is that a tremendous new V–8 engine, the "MEL" of 430 ci (4.29-inch bore and 3.7–inch stroke), was able to accelerate the car from 0 to 60 in under nine seconds. This awesome performance was made possible by 375 bhp and a thundering 490 lb-ft of torque at 3100 rpm. (The same block was used in the Mercury Montclair and with a 4.09 bore was used in the Edsel Corsair, hence "MEL.") Stopping such a monster required new brakes, and the lining area was boosted from 207.5 to 292 square inches. Tires were 9.00x14 on the closed cars and 9.50x14 on the convertibles and air-conditioned cars. The rear axle ratio was dropped to 2.87:1, but the 3.07:1 ratio was retained for the air-conditioned cars.

A more novel feature of this enormous car was the unit body construction, a technique never before used on such a large car. Mac-Pherson pushed this system in order to util-ize the Wixom assembly plant which was prepared for the unit body construction of the new, larger Thunderbird. The initial advantage of unit construction, namely lower weight, was soon lost as reinforcement was added to produce torsional rigidity.

As before, the Lincoln offered two series, the Capri and Premiere, priced about $500 to $600 apart. Three body types were offered: a sedan, a two-door hardtop and a four-door hardtop landau. As usual, Lincoln interiors were sumptuous and of the highest quality.

The fate of the Continental hung in the balance. Stylist John Reinhardt had prepared a clay prototype for a 1958 second-generation Mark II but the sudden decline in sales of the Mark II stopped all development. Reinhart then attempted to modify Najjar's new 1958 Lincoln, but the car was already so large that additional styling bulk in the tradition of the Mark II was impossible.

The company was reluctant to drop the Continental nameplate, so for 1958 the Lin-

The 1958 Mark III Convertible is highly prized by collectors. With the top down, the sight of 20 feet of flat hood and deck evokes images of aircraft carriers. The Mark III remains a marvelous folly and rarity has helped to raise prices to very high levels. *Ford Motor Company*

There are not many surviving 1958 Lincoln Capri four-door hard tops. Only 3,084 were built and, as the Capri was the basic Lincoln, it was overlooked by collectors who sought out the Premiere and the Continental. *Ford Motor Company*

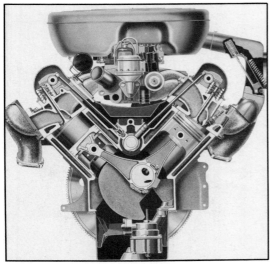

It took a mighty engine to accelerate 5500 pounds to 60 mph in under nine seconds and this great "MEL" block of 430 cubic inches was up to the job. It produced 375 bhp and a whopping 490 pounds feet of torque. The wedge shape combustion chamber has now been achieved with a 10–degree angled block plus a flat head in which valves are flush. Valves and ports are huge. *Ford Motor Company*

coln Continental Mark III name was used on an uptrimmed and slightly restyled Lincoln. It would prove to be a good decision because the Mark III outsold the Premiere. The base price of the Lincoln Premiere four-door sedan was $5,565 while the Mark III was $6,072. For a $500 premium, the reach to the Mark series seemed small and buyers moved up.

The three basic body types of the Capri and Premiere, the two-door and four-door hardtop landau and four door sedan, were offered in the Continental Mark III. Added to the Mark III model lineup was a splendid convertible, a gigantic car much coveted today by collectors. At a base price of $6,283, it was a strong seller in 1958, the 3,048 units second only to the four-door hardtop.

The two Lincoln series and the Continental Mark III were similar in appearance using the same sheet metal. The Continental offered a fine mesh grille and the four-pointed-star hood ornament, but the really distinctive feature was the reverse-angle rear window, used even on the convertible.

For 1959, the Capri and Premiere series were continued. Rather than reuse the Continental Mark III nameplate, Lincoln management called the 1959 Continental, the Mark IV. And in 1960 it became the Lincoln Continental Mark V. It was soon recognized that this was a squandering of a great name. Thus, when the 1961 Continental appeared, the Mark designation was dropped. In 1969, Lincoln management, perhaps hoping that in ten years the 1958 single-year use of the Mark III nameplate had been forgotten, reused the term Mark III on the new personal two-door coupe, a source of confusion.

The 1959 cars were restyled by Don DeLaRossa. The goal was to smooth the body, unclutter the front end and remove the concave side panels. The angularity was muted and the cars were less aggressive in appearance. Compression was lowered from 10.5:1 to 10:1 and horsepower fell back from 375 to 350. The rear axle ratio was 2.89:1.

Two rare body types were introduced in 1959, the Executive limousine and the Formal sedan. A standard sedan was sent to Hess and Eisenhardt in Cincinnati for finishing. All cars were to order.

The limousine had an electrically raised division window. Two radios were fitted for front and rear use. Likewise, two air-conditioning systems were installed, one in the conventional forward location and the second in the trunk for rear passengers. Passenger controls were located in a panel set in the division. The Formal sedan did not have a division. Only a single air-conditioning system and radio were used. Both models had a padded vinyl top, electric door locks and automatic power lubrication. Buyers looking for something very unusual might target these Formal custom cars.

The Capri name was dropped in 1960 and the base model was known simply as "Lincoln." The deluxe Premiere continued.

The rear quarter of the roof was made more conventional on the Lincoln and Premiere and the reverse angle on the side panel was eliminated. But the reverse-angled rear window on the Continental continued. A new dash was introduced with four pods in which were set circular dials. Also for 1960 the coil rear springs were replaced by leaf

The design of the 1959 Mark IV Continental was modified by Don DeLaRossa who softened the angularity, especially noted in the muting of the concave panel behind the front wheel arches.

These big sedans were slow to find collector support and many were lost through junking. This fine example is owned by Grady Jacoway. *Grady Jacoway*

springs which spread the loading on the unit body by doubling the support points. A two-barrel carburetor was used in 1960 to help economy but, horsepower went down to 315 at 4100 rpm while torque was 465 lb-ft at 2200 rpm. The brake lining was thicker. Air conditioning was fitted to 49 percent of the production. Production of the 1960 cars ended earlier than usual to permit major changes for the new 1961 car.

Serial numbers

A new system of numbering with ten digits or letters was used in 1958 and 1959 as follows:

1st—Engine: H = the 430 ci 4-bbl engine, J = 430 ci 6-bbl engine

2nd—Year: 8 = 1958, 9 = 1959

3rd—Plant: Y = Wixom, the new unit body assembly plant

4th—Series and body style: note duplications

    A = 1958 Capri hardtop 2-dr 63A;

    B = 1958 Capri sedan hardtop 4-dr 57A;

    C = 1958 Premiere hardtop 2-dr 63B;

    D = 1959 Premiere hardtop 4-dr 57B

    E = 1958 Continental hardtop 2-dr 65A

    F = 1958 Continental hardtop 4-dr 75A

    G = 1958 Continental convertible 68A

    K = 1958 Capri sedan 4-dr 58A

    L = 1958 Premiere sedan 4-dr 53B

    M = 1958 Continental sedan 4-dr 54A

    A = 1959 Capri hardtop 2-dr 63A, Capri sedan 4-dr 53A, Capri sedan hardtop 4-dr 57A

    B = 1959 Premiere sedan 4-dr 53B, Premiere hardtop 4-dr sedan 57B, Premiere hardtop 2-dr 63B

    C = 1959 Continental (all)

5th—Division: 4 = Lincoln

6th to 10th—Production numbers: 5 digits

Another system of eleven digits and letters was introduced in 1960 which continued through 1975.

1st—Year: 0 = 1960, 1 = 1961 etc. through 1975.

2nd—Plant: Y = Wixom; S = Allen Park, Mich., a pilot plant

3rd—Series: 6 = Lincoln, 7 = Premiere, 8 = Continental

The 1959 Mark IV four door hardtop showed well in dark colors which set off the chrome trim. These cars can still be bought at very reasonable prices but the market moves upward. *Ford Motor Company*

The differences between the 1959 on the left and the 1960 on the right are seen in the picture. For 1960 the front bumper received a new styling focus, more conventional than in 1959 but with two protruding bumper pods. *L.C.O.C.*

This 1960 Mark V two door was offered for $195 in 1972 in San Rafael, California. It was probably junked after one more sale, the fate of so many of these large cars. Sedan prices languished through the seventies but the convertible market began to pick up. *Tim Howley*

4th—Body style (after 1961): 2 = Sedan, 6 = Convertible

5th—Engine: A = 460 ci 4 bbl (1969 to 1976) B&S 4.36x3.85; G = 462 ci 4 bbl (1966 to 1968) B&S 4.375x3.828; H = 430 ci 4 bbl (1958 to 1965) B&S 4.297x3.703; S = 400 ci 2 bbl (began in 1977)

6th to 11th—Production numbers: 6 digits

Production

1958 Capri	
53A 4-dr sedan	1,184
57A 4-dr hardtop	3,084
63A 2-dr hardtop	2,591
Premiere	
53B 4-dr sedan	1,660
57B 4-dr hardtop	5,572
63B 2-dr hardtop	3,043
Continental	
54A 4-dr sedan	1,283
65A 2-dr hardtop	2,328

A fine 1960 Continental Mark V four door showing the reverse angle rear window. These are now finding growing collector enthusiasm but still lag far behind the convertibles. *L.C.O.C.*

The 1960 Mark V convertible has survived in greater numbers than the 1958 and 1959 models. Prices are rising steadily. *L.C.O.C.*

68A 2-dr convertible	3,048
75A 4-dr hardtop	5,891
Total	29,684
1959 Capri	
53A 4-dr sedan	1,312
57A 4-dr hardtop	4,417
63A 2-dr hardtop	2,200
Premiere	
53B 4-dr sedan	1,282
57B 4-dr hardtop	4,606
63B 2-dr hardtop	1,963
Continental	
23A Executive limousine	49
23B Formal sedan	78
54A 4-dr sedan	955
65A 2-dr hardtop	1,703
68A 2-dr convertible	2,195
75A 4-dr hardtop	6,146
Total	26,906
1960 Lincoln	
53A 4-dr sedan	1,093
63A 2-dr hardtop	1,670
57A 4-dr hardtop	4,397
Premiere	
53B 4-dr sedan	1,010
63B 2-dr hardtop	1,364
57B 4-dr hardtop	4,200
Continental	
54A 4-dr sedan	807
65A 2-dr hardtop	1,461
75A 4-dr hardtop	6,604
68A convertible	2,044
23A Limousine	34
23B Formal sedan	136
Total	24,820

Problem areas

Time takes its toll on all cars, especially those with automated devices. Club member Grady Jacoway notes some problems in the 1958 to 1960 series. Check the instrument cluster main dial for a crack between the speedometer numerals 50 and 60 caused by an inadequate cluster support bracket. Repair requires finding a fresh dial and then carefully shimming while installing to relieve stress. A hissing sound in the instrument panel connected with the parking brake is caused by vacuum hoses and perhaps a sticking release button. The ignition switch lock may bind, requiring removal and cleanup. Water leaks can occur at windows and at the front door dog leg. Check for rust at the center pillar where water may enter through the hinge openings. Drain hoses for the air conditioner should be inspected for stoppage.

Club member Bob French notes that a peculiar problem is the rupture of the diaphragm inside the power booster for the windshield wipers. This allows oil to pass into the manifold. The resulting smoke at the tailpipe could be misdiagnosed as engine wear.

Market history

The public reception of the 1958 car was mixed and sales were down. However, all of

The 1960 Lincoln four-door hardtop has become very rare. Collectors opted for the Continental Mark V. Prices are slowly moving upward, bringing perhaps 25 percent of the Mark V Convertible. *Ford Motor Company*

The 1960 instrument panel was highly stylized, like the rest of the car. Quality level was high but ergonomics were secondary to style. *Tim Howley*

the luxury makes lost ground in 1958 and though Lincoln suffered, it was not to be compared to the Imperial, which fell very sharply, or the Packard, which would cease production entirely.

Even with restyling for 1959, sales of the Lincoln and Continental continued to drift lower as they would also in 1960. The car was very big and the sharp body angles not only emphasized the bulk but were hostile and repelling to many buyers.

The 1958 to 1960 Lincolns and Continentals fell rapidly in value in the marketplace and by 1963 were only half the price of comparable Cadillacs. The Imperial's resale value was only slightly better than the Lincoln.

By 1966, the retail value of the 1959 Lincoln was only $130 in the Kelley Blue Book; even the 1960 convertible was worth only $700 retail and a mere $425 wholesale. At these prices, junking was relentless and is the principle reason why so very few of these cars have survived.

The rediscovery of the series began in the seventies with the Continental convertibles, but value climbed slowly. These cars were invariably unrestored and prices were in the $1,000 to $2,000 range. Closed cars continued to be viewed as curiosities with little value. Even by 1977 the top price for a Continental convertible was $3,600 and few sedans could command even $2,000.

Very rapid appreciation began at the close of the seventies for the Continental convertible. By the summer of 1983 top prices had broken through $10,000 and were approaching $15,000. But average cars were available for around $5,000 to $7,000. The closed cars were virtually unaffected and remained at the $3,000 to $4,000 level for perfect cars.

This 1960 Mark V two-door hardtop belongs to Robert Follette. This body style makes a nice choice for collectors who want something more personal than the four-door sedan. It has the further advantage of being cheaper and more available than the convertible. *L.C.O.C.*

This is perhaps the most extreme example of the convertible value premium.

Prices continued to move up. In 1986, the top convertibles were in the $15,000 to $20,000 region. Closed car prices followed slowly. Prices stabilized in this region, in part because there were still so very few fully restored cars and the bulk of the sales were of more ordinary cars at substantially lower prices.

The market continued to show modest growth in the late eighties. The convertibles were often appearing in the auctions. During 1988, the best auction prices were about $16,000.

Whether or not the 1958–60 cars will find substantial appreciation in the nineties remains uncertain. It is clear that these have become "cult" cars, somewhat like the big fin Cadillacs. What the Continental convertible market awaits is a very high auction sale, say over $75,000, which will lead the market. That the Continental tastefully avoided the styling excesses of the Cadillacs may actually work against appreciation since collectors of these types of cars seek the bizarre.

This may also explain why the closed cars languish so severely in this market, namely at about 25 percent of the convertible values. These great Continentals are supreme "display" cars. That the Capri and Premiere lines offered no convertibles during this period has hurt the chance of appreciation. Perhaps this is the reason that so few really good closed Lincolns and Continentals appear on the market because so little money is drawn toward restoring.

Thus buyers should seek out the Continental convertible, keeping a close eye on auction results in anticipation of a price breakthrough. Speculation in closed cars will be a riskier strategy with only gradual appreciation. Enthusiasts who revel in the excesses of this extraordinary car will ignore market considerations and drive with much pride and pleasure.

★★★★	Convertibles
★★★	Sedans

1961–65 Lincoln Continental

History

The 1961 Lincoln Continental began to take shape originally as a Thunderbird project in the Special Projects Studio headed by Elwood P. Engel. Eugene Bordinat, who was to become the vice president of styling, was working on a revision of the 1960 car with good results. The Engel Thunderbird was smaller and designed without any contraints imposed by prior models. When Robert McNamara saw the T-bird he saw a possible new Continental and asked for a stretched version, which was quickly produced.

The new Continental was smaller for another reason. The Wixom plant was committed to unit body construction and the T-bird was its principal product. Production economies could be achieved if the new Lincoln could continue to be built at Wixom, especially in greater volume. Also, if the

The extraordinary 1961 Continental which changed the fortunes of the Lincoln Company. This styling masterpiece used a very small greenhouse to create the illusion of size on what was really a compact chassis. It was an entirely different concept from the other luxury competitions'. Depreciation was slow and many were cherished, which has resulted in a good supply available today. *Ford Motor Company*

complex cowl section could be similar to the T-bird, further production economies would ensue. Thus the Continental was held under very tight dimension limits, which would prove to be a major asset.

The wheelbase of the Continental was reduced from 131 inches to 123 inches which eased the torsional rigidity problem. But on this shorter wheelbase the new puzzle was how to project an image of a luxury car against the Cadillac on a 130-inch wheelbase and the Imperial on a 129-inch wheelbase. The styling answers were brilliant, namely the use of very flat body panels without any side ornamentation and a highlight chrome strip at the top of the side panel for emphasis. The greenhouse was kept small and employed curved glass. The stylists very wisely used great restraint in trim and resisted the temptations of the time to slather on chrome. The end result was an extraordinarily elegant design which rendered the bizarre offerings of Cadillac and Chrysler at once obsolete.

The inspired design paralleled efforts by Harold C. MacDonald to produce the best mechanicals ever achieved by the Ford Motor Company. Over one hundred 1960 Lincolns sold to the public were fitted with many projected 1961 engineering improvements and were specially monitored. MacDonald took special pains to quiet body noise, always a problem in unit construction. Interiors reached new quality heights and no effort was spared to see that the car was delivered in perfect condition. Car assembly was me-

The stylist desire for a beautiful and compact greenhouse led to the use of curved glass windows in the 1961 sedan, expensive but an indication of relentless search for perfection. *Ford Motor Company*

Because of the small greenhouse, space was at a premium. The air conditioning duct was concealed by a central panel which was dropped when in use. When buying these cars, check air conditioning functioning. *Ford Motor Company*

The use of a grille at the rear of the car was another novelty in the 1961 car. *Ford Motor Company*

ticulous with one car a day pulled off the line for examination of tolerances against a master jig. One car per week was torn apart for inspection. Each car was delivered with a two-year, 24,000-mile guarantee, far in excess of the usual ninety-day 4,000-mile standard industry warranty.

There were two body styles—a sedan and a four-door convertible. The convertible was a tremendous novelty and the exceptionally neat top stowage added to the glamour. The complex convertible mechanism, including eleven motors, relays and actuating switchwork, was first used in the 1957 Ford Skyliner. The rear door window automatically lowered when the door was opened.

The engine was carried over from 1960. The 430 ci unit now produced 300 bhp and was coupled to the Twin Range Turbo Drive automatic transmission. A two-barrel carburetor, first fitted in 1959, was used to help fuel economy. Tire sizes were 9.00x14 on the sedans and 9.50x14 on the convertible.

The 1961 models were introduced on November 1, 1960, and received enthusiastic reviews from the press. Sales however were modest, about at the same level as the 1960 model. Production was slow because of the start-up efforts at quality control. Also, the Continental was delivered fully equipped which, to the public, seemed to suggest a $1,000 premium over the Cadillac 62. The public was not exactly pouring through Lincoln showrooms in 1959 and 1960, and it took a while for the Continental to be discovered.

The new Continental was heavy, several hundred pounds over both Cadillac and Imperial, the ironic penalty of unit body construction which was introduced long before as a method to reduce weight by doing away with the separate frame. Performance in both braking and acceleration was below both Cadillac and Imperial. Zero to sixty time was 11 seconds, not bad for a 5,200-pound car. Top speed was around 115 mph. Gasoline mileage was in the 12 to 14 mpg range.

There was remarkable stability in the design of this great Continental. Only minor styling changes were made in 1962. The cen-

There were very few changes in the 1962 Continental. There is no market difference in the prices from 1961 to 1964 and buyers usually seek condition before year. *Ford Motor Company*

Only a few changes again marked the 1963 Continental. This fine example belongs to Raymond Klimczuk. *L.C.O.C.*

The Continental convertible remains the target collectible in the sixties. The popularity of this model continues. Buyers should make sure that the top mechanism is in good order because it is a complex and expensive item to repair. Prices for these splendid convertibles generally run two to three times the price of sedans. *L.C.O.C.*

Two 1964 Continentals, the convertible virtually identical to the 1961 car. Sharp eyed enthusiasts note the subtle differences in the sedan greenhouse. *L.C.O.C.*

80

ter bar in the grille was removed and the bumper was simplified. Power vent windows, automatic headlight dimmer, rear electric antenna and a remote control deck release were helpful improvements. The concealed air-conditioning duct system was eliminated.

For 1963 an alternator was introduced to replace the 1961's generator and engine bhp went up to 320. A new AM-FM radio was in step with the times. There was an aluminum front brake drum now on the sedan as already used on the convertible. The universal joints were strengthened.

The wheelbase on the 1964 Continental was lengthened to 126 inches and this space was used to provide additional room for the rear passengers. An automatic parking release brake, a vertically adjustable steering wheel, and a low fuel warning light were added, among other nice touches. Tire size changed to 9.15x15 on new rims. In 1965, splendid front disc brakes were fitted, sorely needed because weight was climbing and the convertible now was a hefty 5,720 pounds. (There may have been some disc brakes on late 1964 models, according to Wes Joplin). A transistorized ignition system was fitted.

The 1965 Continental was the final flowering of the original slab side design and a convenient break point because not only would the Continental be restyled in the following year, but new products would change the nature of the company.

Tim Howley, editor of *Continental Comments* (#167) reports that perhaps six or eight dual cowl custom phaetons were made by Allan Smith from convertible sedans in San Rafael, California. The vintages would be about 1964 through 1967. These were done without factory authorization but were finished to a high standard.

A 1961 Lincoln convertible (1Y86H405950) was used as the basis for the "Kennedy Lincoln." The car was sent to the Hess and Eisenhardt Company in Cincinnati where the chassis was extended to a 156-inch wheelbase. The car, call SS-100-X or X 100, was delivered to the White House on June 14, 1961. This car weighed 7,800 pounds and was twenty-one feet long. The rear seat could be raised 10½ inches. Equipment was lavish and included two radio telephones.

Following President Kennedy's assassination on November 22, 1963, the X-100 was returned to Hess and Eisenhardt in December where it was armored and fitted with a bulletproof glass roof. A new tuned engine with higher horsepower was fitted to cope with new weight of nearly 10,000 pounds. A special urethane foam was used in the gas tanks to prevent explosions. President Johnson had the car repainted black. Further modifications were made in 1967 and it continued in service until 1977. It is presently at the Ford Museum. A replica has been constructed by club member Kevin N. MacDonald.

Identification

The following Continental styling treatments can quickly identify the year:

1961—Bumper guards and a strong central bar that dips below headlamps
1962—Straight bumper below headlamps

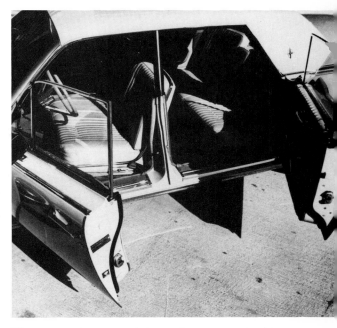

The expensive curved door glass gave way to flat glass in 1964. Rear door edges were more angular. *Ford Motor Company*

with a thin horizontal bar in center of grille

1963—Egg-crate grille with no center bar

1964—Vertical bars on the grille

1965—Flat vertical grille and large parking lamp at apex of front fender above bumper.

Serial numbers

In addition to the codes given in the prior section, the body code for the Continental (the third and fourth digits) are:

53 = 1961 and 1962 4-dr sedan

74 = 1961 and 1962 4-dr convertible sedan

82 = 1963 and up 4-dr sedan

86 = 1963 to 1967 4-dr convertible sedan

The color codes on the warranty plate (directly under the word "Color") for the Continental are as follows:

A = Black satin

C = Princeton gray

E = Silver blue

F = Powder blue

G = Buckskin

H = Nocturne blue

J = Fiesta red

M = Arctic white

N = Platinum

O = Silver green

Q = Huron blue

R = Encino yellow

S = Highlander green

T = Desert sand

U = Regal turquoise

W = Rose

X = Royal maroon

Z = Silver sand

The 1965 convertible still retains the styling of the 1961 car and sales were the highest of the five year period. Owner Hank Pittman enjoys himself in the sun. *L.C.O.C.*

The 1963 Continental convertible retained the superb simplicity of the 1961 car. This factory photo shows the car on the turntable, the stark white background brilliantly contrasted with the black car. The timeless beauty of this design continues to draw collectors. *Ford Motor Company*

The new 1961 Continental looked good from any angle. The four-door sedan was so compact that it could well have been a two door. *Ford Motor Company*

If there is no paint code letter, a special color to customer's choice was used.

Production

1961	Sedan	22,303
	Convertible	2,857
	Total	25,160
1962	Sedan	27,849
	Convertible	3,212
	Total	31,061
1963	Sedan	28,095
	Convertible	3,138
	Total	31,233
1964	Sedan	32,969
	Convertible	3,328
	Total	36,297
1965	Sedan	36,824
	Convertible	3,356
	Total	40,180

Problem areas

Electrical problems are possible with Lincolns of this period, especially with aging. Power door windows can fail, caused sometimes by broken wires at the hinge conduit where they continually flex and even stretch. This especially would be true if the driver's window fails. There is a circuit breaker for the window power system which can disable all windows.

The ammeter itself can fail, especially on the early models, and may appear burnt. Old wiring and loose connections can take their toll.

It is essential that the power top be fully tested. It is an exceptionally complex system requiring eleven relays, four reversible motors, five circuit breakers, two hydraulic cylinders, plus switches. If the system does not work, the top should not be hand operated which could cause further damage. Repairs could be time-consuming and expensive. A description of this system is given in *Continental Comments* #137. A troubleshooting procedure is proved by Ron Baker in #166.

The vacuum door locks should be tested and may sometimes be disabled. The vacuum lines are behind the left kick panel and were too short. They commonly work loose.

Market history

The steadily growing sales success of the Lincoln Continental was a refreshing change from prior Lincoln models and sales reached an initial peak in 1966. It was a splendid showing and reflected continuing buyer support. The used Lincoln market responded appropriately. In 1965, the 1961 sedan and convertible were both retailing around $1,855, for the first time beating Cadillac in both the 62 and De Ville models which were retailing for about $1,495. It was a happy moment for Lincoln management.

Two years later, early Continental values were on a par with Cadillac, year for year. The four-door convertible was valued slightly lower than the sedan in accordance with normal used car depreciation.

By 1972, the early Continental sedans were still selling well, around $1,000 for most models. After the end of the four-door convertible in 1967, all convertibles moved into the collecting category rather quickly and prices began to rise. Thus by the mid-seventies, the convertible was approaching $5,000.

Few were junked and the supply remained good. In the early eighties, prices for convertibles were around $7,000 and remained somewhat flat, perhaps because of abundant supply. A sale in January 1983 offered a 1964 convertible for $12,000. Also, there was speculation in the early eighties on the convertibles which faded about 1984 and caused price flatness. About 1986, appreciation began again with top values moving up to about $10,000 to $11,000. The convertible

market continued to move into the lower and mid-teens as the nineties decade unfolded.

The sedan market has lagged far behind, from 30 to 50 percent of convertible values. The abundant supply of these durable and beautifully made cars has forestalled speculation. Original owners still turn up with treasured veterans. Once again, the ownership of these large and rather costly to operate cars is a function of personal display since collecting rarity is hardly a factor. Thus the convertibles remain at a premium.

The Lincoln Continental is a splendid balanced automobile and can give much pleasure. For this model in particular, collectors should follow the well-worn path to the four-door convertibles for best insurance in the future.

This 1961 presidential limousine was returned to Hess and Eisenhardt in Cincinnati after the Kennedy assassination and rebuilt in the form shown here. Bullet proof glass was added at the rear. *Ford Motor Company*

★★★★	Convertibles
★★★★	Limousines
★★★	Two-door hardtops
★★	Sedans

1966–71 Lincoln Continental and Limousines

History

The Lincoln Continental for 1966 was the first major restyling of the 1961 car. The slab side was modified with a break line near the top and the turn signals were nestled back in the bumpers. The wheelbase was extended to 126 inches.

The 462 ci engine was a bored and stroked version of the reliable eight-year-old 1958 "MEL" 430 ci unit. It produced 340 bhp and drove through a Turbo Drive automatic. Torque was at 485 lb-ft, enough to get the big car up to 60 mph in under eleven seconds, good going for a car of over 5,000 pounds. A low 2.8:1 axle ratio was standard with a 3:1 ratio optional.

A two-door hardtop was added to the line-up to compete against the Cadillac Eldorado. It was a good-looking car and first year calendar sales of 15,766 (model sales 11,080) indicated that a smart decision had been made. In fact, 1966 was the best year ever for Lincoln.

In 1967, the Lincoln Continental had very few changes. Slim vertical bars set off the grille. The convertible was in its last year and sales of only 2,275 units confirmed that this great design was at an end.

For 1968, the parking lights returned to the former location above the bumper tips in the leading edge of the front fender. The Continental star was removed from the top of the hood and placed flush against the front face. The two-door greenhouse was changed; the rear window was smaller and sculptured out of the roof panel more like the new Mark III. Stereo decks appeared in the radios as Lincoln edged toward "sound systems." Horsepower continued at 340 and 485 lbs-ft of torque.

For 1969, the grille was heavily revised with a small rectangular Mercedes-type bar pattern. The new Cadillac paid Lincoln the compliment of copying both frontal and slab side themes. The 460 ci (code A) engine replaced the 462 ci (code G) engine. Though

The 1966 Continental was restyled with a break-line in the side slab panel. The wheelbase was increased to 126 inches. The big 462 ci engine produced 340 bhp with 485 lb. ft. of torque. This sedan belongs to Claude Nordgren. *L.C.O.C.*

the displacement was about the same, the new engine was the largest version of the "385" series, which had come into use in 1968 as a clean-burning anti-smog unit. This was the same basic block as used in the 429 Boss and Cobra Jet series in the Ford. It was a tough high-performance engine. In the Continental it produced 365 bhp and 500 lbs-ft of torque.

In 1970 the Lincoln abandoned the unit body construction and began using perimeter frame. Wheelbase was extended to 127 inches; more overall length was ahead because the Mercury Marquis in 1969 was

New for 1966 was the two-door hardtop, a style which broadened the Continental's appeal. Collectors have confirmed the wisdom of the move; two door prices generally run slightly higher than those of the comparable sedans. J. W. Silviera owns this car. *L.C.O.C.*

The convertible continued in 1966 and was as handsome as ever. Some collectors prefer these later examples; others prefer the earlier slab sided models. The market does not give a clear signal. *L.C.O.C.*

In the second year of production (1967), the two-door hardtop had minor styling changes, most notable the fine vertical accent bars in the grille. The stylized medallion was removed from the front fender. The owner of this car is Gordon Provis. *L.C.O.C.*

longer than the Lincoln! With the new frame, coil springs returned at the rear. Weight dropped 300 pounds.

The headlights were hidden and the parking lamps went back down into the bumper. Wind wings were abandoned. The rear door, four inches wider, was hinged on the middle B-pillar. The whole rear of the car was larger and higher, perhaps reflecting the styling of the Mark III.

In 1970, emission controls really began to take effect and evaporative devices were standard. California cars were fitted with a nitrous oxide control system. Though horsepower ratings were not formally reduced, performance would begin to decline.

For 1971, radial tires were standardized as well as air conditioning, but other changes were minimal. Horizontal bar themes were used in the grille.

Lehmann-Peterson limousines

The Lehmann-Peterson limousines were custom built on Sawyer Avenue in Chicago. First announcement was in May 1963 and the prototype was completed in November using a new 1964 chassis. The wheelbase was stretched to 160 inches. They were Lincoln cataloged beginning in 1966. The initial base price was $13,400 and by 1968 had

Here is the last version of the great four-door convertible It still looks terrific and the very compact greenhouse is about the same size as would have been the case if only two doors had been used. This fine example belongs to Gordon Harbuck. *L.C.O.C.*

risen to $15,104. Numerous options could bring the price to around $20,000.

Production was as follows:

1964—One prototype limousine
1965—Over 100 units delivered by October 1965
1966—101 limousines
1967—85 limousines, one formal sedan
1968—56 limousines
1969—85 limousines

1970—17 limousines, one Town Car and one Mark III 4–dr

Identification

The following styling treatments can quickly identify the year:

Parking lamps	Grille
1966—in bumper	fine horizontal bars
1967—in bumper	5 vertical accents in fine horizontal bars
1968—in fender	3 vertical accents in fine horizontal bars
1969—in fender	Mercedes-type mesh
1970—in fender	4 heavy horizontal bars
1971—in bumper	6 heavy horizontal bars

A Mercedes influence is seen in the 1969 grille with the rectangular bar patterns. There is also a slight center elevation of the grille, a theme which would be further developed. Values for these later Continental sedans are rising slowly. *Ford Motor Company*

The center hump in the hood of this 1970 Continental is developing and crying out for a traditional grille. The Mark III and IV influence continued through the seventies. The roof line of this two-door coupe has been smoothed. This is the first year of the perimeter frame and the wheel base was increased one inch, to 127 inches. *Ford Motor Company*

The 1971 Continental showed minor styling changes. Air conditioning was now standard along with radial tires. There are still some of these tough cars in use and they may often be purchased at modest prices. *Ford Motor Company*

There is little outward difference between this 1970 sedan and its predecessor. The slab sides have lost the upper highlight indentation. *Ford Motor Company*

The 1971 Lincoln Continental coupe was a very smooth design, though there is a lot of mass over the rear wheel arch area. *Ford Motor Company*

This 1969 presidential limousine was delivered on October 14, 1968. The opened center section allowed standing during parades. Secret Servicemen could stand on the rear platform and grasp the hydraulically raised handrail. The platform could be folded upward to become the bumper. *Ford Motor Company*

Serial numbers

Positive identification of the year can be made by the first digit of the serial number: 6 = 1966, 7 = 1967, 8 = 1968, and so on.

Production

1966	4-dr sedan	35,809
	2-dr hardtop	15,766
	convertible	3,180
	Total	54,755
1967	4-dr sedan	32,331
	2-dr hardtop	11,060
	convertible	2,276
	Total	45,667
1968	4-dr sedan	29,719
	2-dr hardtop	9,415
	Total	39,134

The interior of 1969 presidential limousine was finished in silver-gray pinstripe cloth with carpet in silver mouton. *Ford Motor Company*

Production

1969	4–dr sedan	29,258
	2–dr hardtop	9,032
	Total	38,290
1970	4–dr sedan	28,622
	2–dr hardtop	9,073
	Total	37,695
1971	4–dr sedan	27,346
	2–dr hardtop	8,205
	Total	35,551

Problem areas

Reliability increases with years of production. The strong commitment to perfection which marked the opening of this series in 1961 continued and these later Lincoln Continentals are very dependable. The engine change in 1969 to the 460 ci unit (the "385" series) was an answer to growing smog controls but emission controls began to take serious effect in 1970 and may present some tuning problems. Reference should be made to the problem areas of the preceding series for general comment.

Market history

The normal depreciation of these second generations Lincoln Continentals was low until the fuel crunch in 1974 when the bottom fell out of the luxury market. Between the fall of 1974 and 1975, prices fell by 30 percent. Even the Mark III was hurt. But after the big drop, prices stabilized in the mid-seventies and the typical used price for a 1970 or 1971 Continental was around $2,000. Many of these cars were near new. They passed imperceptibly into collectible status, at about the $2,000 level, and slowly gained about 7 percent a year into the early eighties to a top value of about $3,000 for #1 condition cars.

As the cars aged, more appeared in good original #3 condition and many were available for $1,000 in 1982–83. The market

This 1969 Lincoln Town Sedan was a custom show car and used the Mark III headlight covers.

The splendid traditional open front works beautifully. *Ford Motor Company*

advanced slowly into the mid-eighties with prices for top examples breaking $5,000 by 1986. In 1989, prices continued to move upward at the 7 percent rate with perfect cars in the $6,000 to $7,000 region. A more typical sale at the close of the eighties was in the $4,000 to $5,000 area since hardly any of these cars had been subject to restoration.

Auction sales were very sparse because the Lincoln Continental was too often perceived as an old, big and often worn-out car rather than as a collectible. The 1967 convertible remains the standout exception with top condition prices in the mid-teens. The two-door model sells at a 5 to 10 percent premium.

The prospects for this car in the nineties are mixed. There are several questions to answer: 1) Will prices reach the point to justify substantial restoration? 2) Will young collectors be drawn to this model? 3) Will there come a point when rarity motivates collecting? Unless some of these factors are answered positively, appreciation should continue at about the 7 percent level, essentially at an inflation defensive level.

The Lincoln Continental of this period, especially before the smog controls, remains a fast and wonderful car—strong and comfortable, with every conceivable accessory, perhaps the best expression of the great American luxury car. Lincoln was capturing the luxury market from Cadillac step by step and doing it on quality. For those who appreciate this moment in automotive history, these great sedans and two doors have much to offer.

The Lehmann-Peterson limousines remain a special collector category and have found many enthusiastic owners. Prices will be strong, especially for the pristine examples which may still be found. Be on the lookout for the lavish equipment options, especially the nine-inch television set, the beverage unit, reading lights and the intercom system, all expensive items.

Chapter 10

★★★★   All

1968–71 Continental Mark III

History

Marketing studies in 1963 and 1964 confirmed the opinion of Lincoln management that a two-door body was essential in competing against Cadillac. The 1963 estimate was that 4,500 units or 14 percent of Lincoln production would be two-doors—an estimate which would turn out to be very low. A further question was whether or not a two-door Lincoln would impinge on the Thunderbird market, especially since both cars would be built in the Wixom plant and shared some fundamental cowl dimensions.

Development on the new two door began at once under the direction of L. David Ash in September 1965. It was based on the forthcoming 117-inch Thunderbird perimeter frame which would appear in 1967. As in the 1961 Lincoln Continental, the Thunderbird's cowl section was used. The new car, code named Lancelot, had distinctive and brilliant styling features. The upper back panel behind the rear window was two inches higher than the Thunderbird, giving a hunched look. The hood was very long and the side panels very high. The Thunderbird roof and A pillar were used but were hardly noticeable amid the new proportions. The grille was an echo of the Rolls-Royce, hinted at in the press release of February 1968 which made allusions to the British term "motorcar." It was Lee Iacocca who suggested the radiator shape as well as the Con-

The great Mark III is one of the focal points of the Lincoln and Continental Owner's Club. This very popular car continues to win new friends. Handsome, very usable, and modern in an unusual compact specification, the Mark III is champion. Here is a row of Mark IIIs at the 1989 Lake San Marcos meet in California. *L.C.O.C.*

tinental hump on the rear deck. Lush and creative interiors matched the overall styling.

Engineering featured the new 460 ci engine putting out 365 bhp and 500 lb-ft of torque. The compression ratio was 10.5:1. This was the largest version of the "385" series, a clean-burning anti-smog engine which would achieve fame as the 429 Cobra Jet and Boss engine in the Fords. Since the Mark III would weigh 4,738 pounds, down from the Continental weight of 5,093 pounds, performance was up and zero to sixty was 8.3 seconds, an awesome figure even at the reduced weight. The Dual-Range automatic transmission was used with a 2.8:1 axle ratio.

The car was named the Continental Mark III despite the fact that the name had been used in 1958. Marketing people, in a survey, discovered a positive public response to Mark VI; especially to the use of the word, not the number. "Mark" seemed to say "expensive, sporty, prestigious." They then reasoned that a mark number should not be squandered as a single-year designation but as a model designation. This would follow the practice of the Bentley Mark VI and the Jaguar Mark V and Jaguar VII through X. The fact that Bentley had used Mark VI as recently as 1952, and that Jaguar had skipped VI for that reason, may have been another factor.

The car was announced on February 12, 1968, and sales were brisk. By summer, management knew it had a hit and production soared. The spring introduction made sharp model year identification awkward and it was hoped that the car would escape the annual changes. For 1970, the mechanics of the Mark III were virtually identical. An

The original press release photo introducing the Mark III on February 13, 1968. The terrific design was augmented by the new 460 ci engine, powerful enough to haul the 4,738 pound car from zero to 60 mph in 8.3 seconds. This block, from the "385" series would also power Ford's 429 Cobra Jet and big-block Boss engines. Here was a car that had everything and its popularity has continued to this day. *Lincoln-Mercury Division*

evaporative emission control was added for California cars. A Sure Track braking system moderated lockup with a four cycle per second on-off application. Michelin 225R15 radial tires were used, the hubcap design was changed and genuine wood replaced appliquéd trim.

For 1971 the Mark III received a 3:1 rear axle, up from 2.8:1. Though power ratings were the same, emission controls were beginning to strangle the big 460 ci engine and, of course, weight was slowly climbing. Sales were climbing too and in 1971, the Mark III sales of 27,091 nearly equaled the Eldorado's sales of 27,368. But the Eldorado line included 6,800 convertibles so that on a head-to-head coupe competition, the Mark III was the easy victor. There have been a few Mark IIIs customized to convertibles without factory authorization.

The Mark III remained one of the brightest models in Lincoln history.

Identification

The marvelous long hood, small greenhouse and high trunk area quickly identifies the Mark III. The grille is very angular and slightly pointed, with a heavy chrome surround reminiscent of the early thirties.

The 1969 hubcaps have a simulated wire motif. For 1970 the hubcaps are flat. In 1970 the windshield wipers park in a hidden location.

Serial numbers

For the serial number code system, see the plan for the year 1960 in chapter 7. The first number of the serial indicates the year: 9 = 1969, 0 = 1970, and so on.

Colors

There were twenty-two exterior colors offered at the introduction as follows:
A = Black satin

The 1969 Mark III instrument panel was typical of the period: highly stylized, neatly laid out, form more important than function. *Ford Motor Company*

There was very little change in the 1970 Mark III. Collectors like all Mark IIIs and prices are strong. *Ford Motor Company*

M = Arctic white
B = Royal burgundy
Z = Eton gray
L = Foxcroft silver
N = Platinum
X = Admiralty blue
Q = Huron blue
V = Daulton blue
J = Mediterranean
U = Teal
R = Grenoble green
I = Aspen green
H = Cameo green
Y = Chancery gold
E = Antique beige
6 = Desert sand
P = Champagne
G = Belmont green
S = Ascot gray
W = Mikado yellow
C = Dark yellow green metallic

The vinyl roof trim was either black or parchment on all models. Dark ivy gold was also recommended for the four green colors.

The Posi-traction rear axle was offered and can be quickly identified on the warranty plate along with the axle ratio. Look in the space under "axle" for a letter or number. Use the following code:

5 = Conventional axle ratio 3:1
3 = Conventional axle ratio 2.8:1
0 = Conventional axle ratio 2.5:1
E = Posi-traction axle 3:1

C = Posi-tracton axle 2.8:1

Production
1968— 7,770
1969—23,088
1970—21,432
1971—27,091
Total—73,381

Problem areas
The Mark IIIs were in the tough Lincoln tradition and many have run up very high mileages with little trouble.

Check the trunk area for moisture, especially under the trunk lid. Condensation can be the problem, as can plugged hoses from vent box of the flow-through air system. A clunk in the rear end may be nothing more than a loose lower control arm.

Market history
The Mark III was aimed at the Cadillac Eldorado and in four short years it succeeded in establishing sales parity. New prices were virtually identical during this period. In the used car market, the Mark III easily bested the Eldorado, a fine triumph for Lincoln. At the end of 1973, a 1969 Mark III could command $4,000, well up from the Eldorado's $3,655.

The Mark III was a triumph in another way. It was one of those rare cars that was seen as a collecting piece as soon as production ended. This is all the more remarkable because it was not offered as a convertible. Thus, in the mid-seventies, the Mark III's value bottomed out somewhere around $2,500 and then began to climb. Owners were reluctant to part with this car and many have remained in original hands, especially when price acceleration became obvious.

In the early eighties, Mark III prices moved up to around $5,000, well ahead of comparable Eldorado values. By 1986, the best examples were moving rapidly upwards to around $9,000. At the end of the eighties some price stability was seen around $10,000. This may have been caused by a large pool of cars coupled with the inevitable supply of fresh cars emerging from estates of deceased loyal owners.

This 1971 Mark III is owned by Vern McGuire. Though there were few changes in three model years, be on the lookout for such nice accessories as the posi-traction rear axle. *L.C.O.C.*

This custom built dual cowl phaeton was shown at the Chicago Auto Show on February 21, 1970. The photo is dated January 29, 1970. The top was removed, the interior was retrimmed and there were other sheet metal and grille changes. There have been a few Mark IIIs which have been privately modified into convertible coupes.
Ford Motor Company

Mark IIIs appear in great abundance in the auction market. Most of them are in class #3 condition, namely, very good older original cars showing wear, the sort of car that has been kept over the years by loving owners. At the close of the eighties, these cars were selling in the $3,000 to $4,000 range. The perfectly restored Mark III was rare in an auction and in 1988 had made $15,000.

In the nineties, the Mark III values should steadily advance. The future will depend on the sort of collector who enters the market. Nostalgic older buyers may be less concerned about condition, which will sustain the middle price market. Collectors who are seriously restoring these cars still are rare since so many good original examples can still be found. The Mark III's speculative potential remains limited; there are simply too many cars available. But it is a wonderful personal car to drive and savor and it will give enormous pleasure to new generations.

Chapter 11

1972–76 Continental Mark IV

History

The Continental Mark IV project was directed by Wes Dahlberg. He was provided a new perimeter frame with a 120.4–inch wheelbase, which allowed not only new freedom of development but made possible a more direct response to the Eldorado's 126.3–inch wheelbase. That Ash's Mark III

As is so often the case, the first model of a new design is the purest expression and this is certainly true in this 1972 Mark IV, designed under the direction of Wes Dahlberg. A longer wheelbase gave more scope to Dahlberg who did, however, retain the crispness of the original 1969 Mark III. The 460 ci engine continued but horsepower was dropping as emissions control slowly strangled power. *Ford Motor Company*

had created such a luxury feel on the short 117–inch wheelbase is a tribute to his styling genius.

Dahlberg used crisp and sharp lines, reduced the rear hump, retained the Mark III grille and removed the belt line entirely. A little oval opera window appeared in the rear quarter. The whole ensemble was a masterpiece of balanced, stylistic restraint, yet it had a dramatic impact that turned all heads.

The technical specifications were like the Continental. The rear suspension used coil springs located with four control arms, the whole mounted on the perimeter frame. Steel rails were added to the doors for crash protection and the dash was redesigned for impact safety. Intermittent wipers were specified.

The big 460 ci engine was continued but brake horsepower was radically reduced to an advertised net 212 bhp. The horsepower race was over and the Mark IV no longer was touted as having a horsepower advantage over the Continental.

The rivalry of the Mark IV with the Eldorado continued and *Motor Trend*'s annual "King of the Hill" comparison continued to charm readers. The Mark IV for 1972 received highest marks for styling and general luxury while the Eldorado won on performance. The public voted for the Mark IV which handily beat Eldorado sales. The Mark

IV also beat Continental sales for the first time and would maintain that dominance through 1974.

In 1973, federal regulations demanded new impact absorbing bumpers, 5 mph at the front and 2½ mph at the rear. Massive bumpers appeared on the Mark IV which gave the car a front heavy look. This required that the parking lights be restyled and enlarged but few other changes were made. Additional smog controls included a recirculating exhaust gas system. Performance was little enhanced even though horsepower was rated at 219 with 360 lbs-ft of torque. The radial tire size was increased to 230x15 or LR78x15. The new side terminal battery size was reduced from eighty-five to seventy-five amperes while the alternator rating went up from fifty-five to sixty-five amperes. The battery was need only for starting.

Sales success for the Mark IV in 1973 was phenomenal, a record 69,437 units. The Eldorado sold 42,136 coupes and 9,315 convertibles. Cadillac dominance of the prestigious personal car market was over.

There were some changes in the 1974 Mark IV. Further emission controls now included a belt-driven pump to inject air into the engine to mix with unburned hydrocarbons. With the pump were check valves, anti-backfire valves, rubber hoses and the air distribution manifold system. Horse-

For 1973, the new bumpers were bulky in order to meet federal impact regulations. The parking lamps were no longer integrated into the bumper tip design and were enlarged. This would be a peak sales year for the Mark IV. Randolph Scott owned this 1973 Mark IV. *L.C.O.C.*

power dropped to 215. For comparison, the big 500 ci Cadillac engine, which was proudly advertised at 365 bhp in 1971, was now down to an SAE net 210 bhp. The new power brake system was used in the Mark IV, a sophisticated and welcomed improvement.

A very irritating federal regulation required the starter interlock in 1974 in which seat belts had to be fastened before the engine would start. If the driver failed in the drill, a warning light and buzzer appeared when the key was inserted. The system was disabled by the thousands and it was one of the few regulations which was revoked through noncompliance.

It is sad that as horsepower was declining, weight was climbing. The jump was particu-

Collectors will be on the lookout for the glass-panel moonroof shown in this 1973½ Mark IV. The panel was electrically powered and had a silver reflective surface which gave one-way vision. Any accessory which can set a Mark IV apart from the standard offerings will enhance value. *Lincoln-Mercury Division*

The 1974 Mark IV had few exterior changes but a maintenance free battery was introduced. Horsepower was now down to 215 and 10 miles per gallon was about normal. A belt driven pump injected air to mix with unburned hydro-carbons. The first big fuel price increase was just beginning. Maintenance was becoming more complicated. This might have an effect on prices—favoring the earlier models. But condition is everything when buying any collector car. *Ford Motor Company*

The length of the Mark IV is evident in this factory picture of the 1975 model. A standout feature for this year was four wheel disc brakes. Prices were going up sharply, to well over $11,000; gasoline touched 60¢ per gallon. Sales went down to 47,145 units. *Lincoln-Mercury Division*

larly noticeable in the Mark IV which went from 4,908 pounds in 1973 to 5,362 pounds in 1974.

The 1974 Mark IV received minor styling and convenience touches. An illuminated vanity mirror appeared in the sun visor with two-level intensity lighting. The battery was maintenance free (sealed). The fuel capacity was raised 4 gallons to 26.6 gallons and a new left quarter panel filler replaced the one behind the license plate. The big fuel tank was needed because fuel consumption was around 10 mpg.

Gasoline prices became a problem for the first time in 1974 and buyers were conscious of fuel costs. Sales of the Mark IV dropped to 57,316, still a tremendous achievement but the peak had been reached.

This front quarter view of the 1975 Mark IV shows that it was not much different from the 1974 model. *Ford Motor Company*

The interior of the Mark IV was sumptuous. The loose cushion effect of the seat design was not unlike that of the finest coachbuilders of the twenties. *Ford Motor Company*

In 1975, the catalytic muffler appeared on California cars and was fitted to around half of all production for the other states. Horsepower in the Lincoln was actually raised to 220 with dual exhausts. The 500 ci Cadillac produced only 190 SAE net bhp. The axle ratio was raised from 2.75:1 to 3:1 in the California cars. The Mark IV was given four-wheel disc brakes, a splendid improvement. The tilting steering wheel was standard; door locks and the deck release were power operated. A speed control was standard.

The gasoline crunch was severe in 1975 and prices reached sixty cents per gallon. Buyers took a second look at the big luxury cars with their ten miles per gallon performance. Mark IV sales dropped to 47,145. Another reason for sales resistance was heavy price increases. The following chart tells the story:

1972— $8,640
1973— $8,984
1974—$10,194
1975—$11,082
1976—$12,560 (Designer Series)

The final statement of the Mark IV, this 1976 model is very little changed from its 1972 beginnings. The public was still enchanted and sales went back up to 56,110 cars. The Mark IV, like the Mark III, was seen as a collectible by many owners and depreciation is slow. Collectors will seek out the four special Designer series cars. *Ford Motor Company*

Buyers took time to adjust to these increases and some simply left the market.

For the final year of production, the 1976 Mark IV went out in a blaze of glory with the designer series. Emilio Pucci, Cartier, Hubert de Givenchy and Bill Blass each created color coordinated versions of the Mark IV as follows:

Blass: Dark blue metallic paint, cream landau vinyl roof, cream and gold hood, blue Versailles-styled majestic cloth or blue leather

Cartier: Dove gray paint with red and white hood

Givenchy: Aqua blue diamond fire paint, white landau vinyl roof, black and white hood, aqua blue interior

Pucci: Dark red moondust paint, silver vinyl landau roof, silver and lipstick red hood, dark red interior

These imaginative treatments were only one set of choices. Seven luxury color groups were offered for the last time in 1976. They were blue diamond, saddle and white, lipstick and white, gold and cream, red and rose, dark and light jade, and jade and white. Also available was the Versailles option, soft crushed majestic cloth with a down-filled appearance plus right and left vanity mirrors. Buyers still unmoved could pick diamond fire, moon dust metallic and black diamond paint. The moonroof was also available in five tints: silver, gold, brown,

Many Continental Mark IVs are maintained in concours condition. Roger Martinez is the owner of this 1975 model. With good care and careful use, these cars give splendid service with running costs easily offset by appreciation. *Tim Howley*

light jade or rose. It may have been the most extraordinary color display in Lincoln history.

Mechanical and styling changes were minimal in this last year of Mark IV production. The big 460 ci engine continued, now on an 8:1 compression ratio with a 202 net bhp rating. The EPA fuel consumption rating was 9.5 mpg city and 15.1 mpg on the highway with the 2.75:1 axle ratio. Despite gasoline shortages and rising prices, buyers stepped up for the Mark IV and production totaled 56,110 cars.

Identification

In 1972, the Mark IV had the bumper with the cutout for the grille. In 1973, the massive 5 mph bumper appeared. The exterior features of the 1974 model were unchanged. In 1975 the front bumper guards were set wider apart. Again there were no exterior changes in 1976.

Serial numbers

The Vehicle Identification Number (VIN) always begins with the last digit of the year: 2 = 1972, and so on. It is crucial in dating the Mark IVs because of such minor styling changes.

Production

1972—48,591
1973—69,437
1974—57,316
1975—47,145
1976—56,110
Total—278,599

Market history

One of the more astonishing qualities of the Mark IV is the speed with which it moved into collecting circles. More than any other model, the Mark IV proved that the Lincoln styling and merchandising were so strong that they could establish a permanence of value. This was seen very early by used car dealers. In 1977, the 1972 Mark IV was still able to command $4,000 in the retail market. The Cadillac Eldorado, the direct competitor, was at $3,280. The 1972 Imperial was a poor third with a value of $2,440.

The Mark IVs were seen as "keepers" and, despite the very substantial production, continued to hold value. In 1984, the Kelley Blue Book would still list the 1972 Mark IV at $2,450, the Eldorado at $1,635 and the Imperial at $1,145. The Kelley Blue Book reflected conventional used car depreciation. By this time, collectors were beginning to seek out the car and, in this specialized market, prices were climbing above Kelley estimates with values in the $4,000 to $5,000 region. Original owners quickly picked up on this remarkable situation. Since the early eighties, prices have moved steadily upward with the Mark IV breaking into five figures for exceptional examples at the close of the decade. There is a likelihood that appreciation will continue in the nineties because auctions have already produced some very strong prices for Mark IVs in the $20,000 to $30,000 region. These prices may not reflect normal sales but they are not forgotten and sellers instinctively "move up" in their thinking.

Of the various Mark IVs, the original 1972 model remains the purest design without the heavy bumpers, and some collectors favor it. Likewise, the designer series in the final year, 1976, has many followers and sells at a premium. The 1975 model may have slightly lower value in the eyes of some collectors.

Another factor to consider is the emissions controls which were heaped on these cars year by year. In particular, the air pump was added in 1974 and the catalytic muffler in 1975. Horsepower suffered. Some collectors move toward the earlier models to avoid these complications.

In any event, the Mark IV was a hit in its own time and has remained so. The wonderful luxury of these cars and their steady refinement make them standouts in the luxury market. Slow and steady appreciation is assured.

The front view of the 1973 Mark IV had more than a hint of a Palladian style grille and the effect is splendid. The clean design of all of the Mark series was an important reason for its continuing success. *Ford Motor Company*

Chapter 12

1972–79 Lincoln Continental

History

The tumultuous final eight years of the Lincoln Continental remain one of the fascinating moments in automotive history. At no other time did marketing conditions change so severely.

In 1972, the luxury market seemed to go on forever. Lincoln and Cadillac were fighting it out with the Imperial a poor third. Lincoln was gaining; the great Mark IV would establish leadership in the personal market. No one in Detroit management

The hump in the rear door was moved rearward on the 1972 Lincoln Continental which lengthened the appearance of the car. The folding, standup hood ornamental returned to the front of the hood. The Mercedes style grille treatment returned in greater relief. The new Town Car style was introduced, and collectors who seek four-door sedans usually prefer the Town Car style. *Lincoln-Mercury Division*

The instrument panel on the 1972 car was neatly laid out but legibility and fine accuracy were not top priorities. Circular instruments were still a foreign idiom. *Ford Motor Company*

could have foreseen the fuel crisis in 1974 and 1980. And few took seriously the challenge of the imports, especially the Mercedes which would eventually change the way the public would define luxury.

The Lincoln Continental for 1972 was restyled and did away with the hump at the rear. The upper edge of the rear door panel was straightened and a bright molding appeared on the top edge of the front fender much like the 1961 car. The result was that the bulk of the car seemed reduced. The heavy bar grille of 1971 was abandoned and the Mercedes grille theme was recalled in a rich treatment. The Continental star was again mounted on the hood prow, with a safety mounting that allowed it to deflect under impact.

The new "Town Car" style appeared in 1972, a style that would last. It was a trim option which featured a molding across the car at the B-pillar; the rear half of the roof was padded and an opera light was added at the pillar. The option with leather cost $635.

This 1973 four door sedan was given to Leonid I. Brezhnev on June 18, 1973. There were few changes from 1972 though emissions controls were increased. The impact absorbing bumper was well integrated into the sedan, better than on the Mark IV. *Ford Motor Company*

One was reminded of the town cars of the twenties but the chauffeur in the 1972 Lincoln Continental Town Car was hardly seated in Spartan open air surroundings.

Two convertibles were also built by the factory, one of which has survived in the hands of Victor Born, Jr., of Arizona.

Unleaded gasoline was now part of emissions controls and compression dropped to 8.5:1. Horsepower was no longer an issue and the SAE net now quoted was 212 bhp. Performance was still formidable with a zero to sixty time only 0.3 seconds slower than 1971. Sales took off in 1972 and Lincoln Continental did the best since 1966.

Changes were minor for 1973. The word "Continental" appeared across the hood face. Colors were expanded and sound insulation was increased. More important changes appeared in the emissions control systems which included a closed crankcase ventilating system, a fuel vapor emissions control system and exhaust controls. Fuel-air ratios were changed and ignition was retimed. The nitrous oxide problem was met by an exhaust gas recirculation system which diluted the incoming fuel-air charge. Things were getting complex as engineers struggled to clean

up the great 460 ci engine, yet horsepower rose to 219.

New for 1973 was the 5 mph impact-absorbing front bumper, a massive unit which was better looking on the Continental than on the Mark IV. The rear 2½ mph bumper was even more attractive. Sales continued strong, though down a bit from 1972.

The 1974 Continental continued along proven styling themes. The front grille was now composed of small vertical bars, more like the Mark IV. New and more massive bumpers were required by the federal swinging pendulum impact test; the rear bumpers were now also 5 mph impact proof. Stylists did their best to integrate the bulky units. The roof support was strengthened to meet new federal crush strength standards which mandated a force one and one half times the car weight to be applied to the front edge of the roof without structural failure.

It was a time of maximum federal intervention. Emission controls were ever tighter and in 1974 required a belt-driven air pump to help consume unburned hydrocarbons in the exhaust system and to oxidize carbon monoxide. The system was complex with

The vertical grille bars are the styling feature for 1974. Sales were down because of fears of fuel shortage. Sales for 1974 were the lowest for the 1972–79 era. Rarity appears not to affect collecting value; collectors look first for the pristine low-mileage example of any of these big Lincolns. *Lincoln-Mercury Division*

numerous check valves, anti-backfire valves, hoses and an air distribution manifold. The irritating starter interlock was introduced in 1974 but did not last as angry owners disabled the system. Solid state ignition was used which allowed more precise timing to control emissions and did away with breaker points which, in wearing, would change timing. Weight was up 168 pounds in the Continental to 5,384 pounds, the result of these federal mandates.

A power brake system now used the hydraulic pump of the power steering system which stored fluid under pressure, enough to make several applications with the engine stopped.

Luxury development continued. Sound insulation was added which complimented the steadily improving electronic sound systems. Lincoln interiors continued to lead the industry. The sense of total luxury in the Town Car option was overwhelming.

Times were changing and the fuel shortages appeared in 1974 causing a recession in the luxury market. For the first time, buyers saw risks with the large luxury cars and sales fell 37 percent for the Continental. Another reason was the sharp increase in prices. In

This picture has been very subtly elongated to exaggerate the length of the 1975 coupe with the Landau roof. A close inspection of the wheels reveals they are not round! The car was big enough without exaggeration and this model found 21,185 buyers, a record. Among collectors, the coupe appears to bring a slight premium over the sedans. *Lincoln-Mercury Division*

The 1976 Lincoln was little changed from 1975. This was the last year that 460 ci engine would be offered in California. *Ford Motor Company*

1974 the Continental base price increased $835 (11 percent) from $7,474 to $8,309. This would be followed by another 11 percent increase of $905 for 1975. Even wealthy buyers noticed these increases.

The year 1975 opened on an uncertain note with substantial 1974 inventories which were cleared, with difficulty, through profit-cutting rebates. It is remarkable that Lincoln was able to show progress in this climate, especially when rivals such as the Imperial suffered a crushing decline.

The good news may have been generated by the considerable restyling of the Continental for 1975. Most noticeable was a widening of the B-pillar with a coach lamp option. This "colonnade" style, as used on the two-door coupe, created a new fixed quarter window in which the Continental emblem was laminated. The upper door moldings were omitted and the roof line was now defined by the door opening. The Town Car trim was available in both coupe and sedan. The rear of the car was quite different with new taillamps and a red applique which ran across the entire width of the back panel.

Five extra cost luxury groups were available with color coordination. They were diamond blue, saddle white, silver, gold, and lipstick and white. Buyers found in these groups an easy solution to the puzzle over complex color choices. The Designer Series idea was forming on the horizon.

A catalytic muffler was added to the emission system. California cars received a 3:1 rear axle, while the 2.75:1 was standard elsewhere, though 50 percent of those cars were fitted with the 3:1 option. Four-wheel disc brakes were an extra cost option.

The 1975 Lincoln Continental was a splendid car and perhaps at the very summit of American engineering. The emission controls hobbled the 460 ci engine but it could still haul the 5,400 pound coupe from 0 to 60 mph in 10.5 seconds. The 10 to 12 mpg was a problem but wealthy owners did not flinch. The ride was soft and silent. Power accessories were everywhere.

The coupe was particularly sharp and was an instant hit. It looked much like the Cadillac but if anything, was cleaner in design. The public loved these cars and despite fuel shortages and high prices bought 54,698 Continentals of which 21,185 were coupes.

For 1976, the Continental was virtually unchanged. Even the price held steady, increasing only $79. The Town Car trim

The Mark IV influence is evident in this 1977 Lincoln with a new traditionally styled grille and the landau porthole. The public loved this car and sales reached a thundering 95,600 for the coupe and sedan. Most collectors and appraisers now rate this new look as more desirable than the 1972–76 offerings. *Lincoln-Mercury Division*

option continued. Among the few new options were an opera window for the four-door sedans, aluminum wheels, four-note horn and an engine block heater. Sales boomed along with a total of 68,646 units, 38 percent of the Cadillac de Ville sales, a record for Lincoln. But Cadillac had all-time record sales of 309,139 and 43,772 were the new small Seville. In 1984 the Seville would be selling at 50 percent of its new price while the de Ville (and the Continental) was bringing only about 30 percent of its new price. The market was shifting, favoring the smaller cars.

For 1978, the heavy chrome strip was removed from the lower waist line and the rear fender cut outs were opened up. The simplified look recalls earlier themes of the sixties. The downsized Cadillac was meeting with sales resistance and Lincoln profited. Collectors look for the new Williamsburg options. This was the last year for the 460 ci engine, even now a non-California option over the smaller standard 400 ci engine. *Ford Motor Company*

The last big Lincoln appeared in 1979 and it was a bold gamble as gasoline shortages reappeared. The timing was just about perfect as the Iran oil crisis came in February, 1979. Production was halted in June. The Collector series capitalized on the end of the large cars and buyers turned out. *Ford Motor Company*

This 1972 presidential limousine was built on a 161-inch wheelbase. Various options provided cover for the rear compartment to meet any contingency. *Ford Motor Company*

But not yet. In 1977, the Continental was restyled and given the Mark V grille with an unusually handsome result. Trim was revised and cornering lamps appeared in the lower panel ahead of the front wheels. The Town Car options included vinyl roof, the loose pillow seat trim, coach lamps and power vent windows. Engineers were able to reduce weight through styling simplification.

In California only, a new 400 ci engine was fitted. It was an enlarged 351 Cleveland engine, a fine anti-smog unit with up-to-date canted-valve cylinder head design. A four-barrel carburetor was fitted. The California smog requirements were severe; as an example, hydrocarbons limits were 0.4 gram per mile as compared to 1.5 grams for the federal standard. Carbon monoxide limits were half of the federal standards. To the California 400 ci engine was added a bigger catalytic converter and a Duraspark ignition system. Power output was nearly that of the 460 ci unit.

Apparently, a few 1977 convertibles were customized at a shop at an unknown location (perhaps Washington, DC or Pasadena?), according to club member Ken Nye, and were sold without warranty. They may have used top mechanisms from 1971–72 Ford LTDs.

The interior of the 1972 presidential limousine was trimmed in gray leather. Both a telephone and a microphone for a loudspeaker were fitted. *Ford Motor Company*

Sales zoomed to 95,600, the best year ever for Lincoln. The downsizing of the Cadillac de Ville may have helped sales as luxury car buyers made traditional choices for size. In any event, the Continental sales were now 61 percent of de Ville sales, the highest ever. Including the Mark V, Lincolns sales were 175,921, an all-time record.

The California 400 ci engine became standard for the 1978 Continental. The 460 was still available as an option outside of California. Fleet fuel economy requirements

The 1975 four-door Lincoln Continental had the new power-braking system with optional four-wheel disc brakes. It was a fine automobile and good examples can still be found at very reasonable prices. *Lincoln-Mercury Division*

were 18 mpg in 1978. Though Lincoln was not directly threatened because of offsetting economy in the small Ford cars, the need to reduce weight and increase gasoline mileage was evident. The 400 engine was fitted with a two-barrel carburetor, and used a 2.5:1 axle. Aluminum, thin glass and high strength thinner alloy steels all helped to cut weight. Whereas the 1976 sedan weighed 5,442 pounds, the 1978 sedan weighed 4,661 pounds. EPA mileage went up from 12 mpg in 1977 to 13–15 mpg in 1978.

There were very few styling changes in the 1978 Continental. The Town Car options continued. In addition there was a Williamsburg feature car with some Town Car features, a personal nameplate, special interior lighting and twin comfort lounge seats with recliner. The Williamsburg came in two tu-tone colors: champagne/metallic light champagne and midnight cordovan/dark cordovan. Sales continued strongly, little changed from 1977.

The final year of the big Continental was 1979 and this great car went out in a blaze of glory. The 460 ci engine was no longer available as an option and the 400 ci engine with the two-barrel carburetor was now standard. The Town Car options continued. The Williamsburg Series was expanded to seven tu-tone color combinations: light silver metallic/medium gray metallic, medium turquoise metallic/dark turquoise, light champagne/dark champagne metallic, cordovan metallic/light chamois, light chamois/cordovan metallic, jubilee gold metallic/cream, and cream/jubilee gold metallic (in reverse pattern).

Lincoln made much of the last chance to buy a full-size luxury car, which led to the Collector Series, specially trimmed Town Cars in midnight blue metallic or white, plus turbine style aluminum wheels, gold color grille and a color-keyed vinyl roof. The interiors were in midnight blue. Advertising themes were "full size luxury with classic styling." The last big Cadillac, the Eldorado, was gone and Lincoln made the most of size.

It was a good idea and early sales suggested another hit year. Then the Iranian oil crisis came in February 1979. Lincoln sales continued strong for a while but soon gasoline lines formed in the spring, and sales of the big heavy cars virtually stopped. The Continental production was halted unusually early, on June 8, in the light of massive inventory. Nostalgia for the big cars could not win against the fear of gasoline shortages.

In a sense, Lincoln's timing was nearly perfect. The great Continentals would have sold well throughout the year had it not been for the fuel crisis. But even with the fuel crisis, the phase-out of the big cars was only cut short by a few months and the new 1980 downsized cars were ready for the fall introduction.

Top quality leather was expected in a 1972 Continental. Tilt wheel has been angled down for this driver. The flat seats and backs offer no lateral support but the buyers of luxury cars in 1972 would not have been interested. *Ford Motor Company*

Thus, the traditional Continental production came to a close in June of 1979. Though there was the general sense that the cars may no longer have fit the times, there also was sadness that cars of this dimension and luxury would never again be produced. An era had come decisively to an end.

Serial numbers

First digit indicates year: 1 = 1971, 2 = 1972, and so on.

Second letter indicates plant: Y = Wixom.

Third and fourth numbers indicate the body: 81 = coupe, 82 = sedan.

The fifth letter indicates the engine: A = 460 ci, S = 400 ci.

For example, 2Y81(A)80001 is a 1972 Lincoln Continental coupe with a 460 ci engine.

Production

1972 4–dr sedan		35,561
2–dr hardtop (includes two convertibles)		10,408
Total		45,969
1973 4–dr sedan		45,288
2–dr hardtop		13,248
Total		58,536
1974 4–dr sedan		29,351

	2–dr hardtop	7,318
	Total	36,669
1975	4–dr sedan	33,513
	2–dr	21,185
	Total	54,698
1976	4–dr sedan	43,983
	2–dr	24,663
	Total	68,646
1977	4–dr sedan	68,160
	2–dr	27,440
	Total	95,600
1978	4–dr sedan	67,110
	2–dr	20,977
	Total	88,087
1979	4–dr sedan	76,458
	2–dr	16,142
	Total	92,600

Market history

The Iranian gas crisis of 1979 coincided with the end of the Lincoln Continental production. From the standpoint of product planning, the timing was almost perfect, but by late spring inventory was heavy and, as has been noted, production ended on June 8. The gas crisis had a chilling effect on the used luxury car market.

At the end of 1981, a six-year-old Continental was bringing a meager $2,500 retail and few dealers would offer more than $1,500 wholesale. It was the time when little 1975 Toyota Corollas would bring more. But as the eighties unfolded, prices went no lower. Three years later in 1984, the 1975 Continental was still bringing $2,500. By the late eighties, very little had changed. Inflation made some of this stability an illusion for true values were still declining.

But in this series from 1972 to 1979, certain trends were becoming apparent. Early cars with less smog control and late cars from the Collector and Williamsburg editions were finding collector interest. The Town Car options were helpful in establishing value. Yet the various appraisal guides could find no unanimity of appraisal and offer wildly differing estimates, a sure sign of a thin market. The abundance of these cars, many in the hands of original owners, prevented any sudden appreciation.

It seems unlikely that this rather placid situation will change in the nineties. Collectors have preferred the Mark series over the Continental sedans and coupes. So many good examples remain that restoration is superfluous. Owners often cherish these cars and are indifferent to speculative possibilities. Buyers who choose to find the final and most luxurious expression of American automotive art should look no further.

Chapter 13

1977–79 Continental Mark V

History

The 1977 Continental Mark V was styled by Don DeLaRossa who accented angularity with such touches as a sharply pointed rear quarter window. Three louvers appeared behind the front wheel arch. The wheelbase continued at 120.4 inches but the car appeared even bigger than the Mark IV. The remarkable tribute to new design work was that weight dropped 800 pounds, a splendid achievement in a fuel short environment. Aluminum wheels helped along with a space-saving spare.

The successful Designer Series was continued. The Bill Blass edition continued in midnight blue paint with chamois color vinyl roof and leather. Cartier used dove grey paint with matching roof and leather. Hubert de Givenchy's design was dark jade metallic paint, chamois pigskin grain forward vinyl half roof, dark jade leather and a chamois color hood. Emilio Pucci specified black diamond fire paint, white Cayman grain vinyl roof and white leather. Designer Series cars had a gold-finished instrument panel, right and left vanity mirrors, and the turbine spoke aluminum wheels among other features.

Mechanical specifications were similar to the Mark IV. The 400 ci engine was specified for California, a new engine based on the 335 series, in essence an expanded 351 Cleveland block first introduced in Fords in 1970. It produced 181 bhp. It was a clean-burning anti-smog engine with the canted-valve cylinder head. But with heavy emissions controls, mileage was little better than 10 mpg. The public loved this car and bought 80,321 Mark Vs, a record which easily beat the Eldorado coupe's production of 47,344 units.

The success of the Mark V continued in 1978. The 400 ci engine was now standard throughout the Lincoln line-up. Styling

The 1977 Mark V is posed in front of the earlier Continental Mark series. The original Continental is upper left, the Mark II is left center and the Mark III and Mark IV are at right. The continuity of the Mark III, IV and V is clear. The moonroof is a sought after option and will bring a premium. *Lincoln-Mercury Division*

changes included hubcap designs, minor trim and new color options. The Designer Series had new colors. Bill Blass went from midnight blue to cordovan with matching interiors; Pucci from black diamond fire paint to silver metallic with dark red and dove gray interior leather; Givenchy moved from dark jade to midnight jade with chamois and jade interiors; and Cartier abandoned dove grey for light champagne with matching interiors. The Bill Blass edition had the Carriage Roof, a mock convertible style, which was an option throughout the Mark V line.

The Diamond Jubilee edition was offered with diamond blue metallic or jubilee gold paint with matching interiors. Even at a $20,529 base price, sharply above the Mark V base price of $12,099, the Diamond Jubilee found 5,159 buyers.

The Mark V continued in 1979 with few changes except for sharp price increases. The Designer Series again offered new

The interior of the 1977 Mark V shows the elaborate leather seat design, here in dove grey leather. *Lincoln-Mercury Division*

colors. Bill Blass liked the white mock convertible top with midnight blue paint; Cartier used champagne with dark red trim; Pucci used turquoise exteriors with white interiors; and Givenchy featured a dark blue paint with dark leather.

Sales were strong in the fall until the Iranian fuel crisis in February. The Mark V was less affected than the Continental, but by summer unsold cars were everywhere and distress selling was taking place.

Serial numbers

First number indicates the year: 7 = 1977, and so on.

Second letter indicates the plant: Y = Wixom.

Third and fourth letters indicate body: 89 = Mark V.

Fifth number indicates the engine: S = 400 ci.

For example, 8 (–) 89 (S) 800001 identifies a 1978 Mark V with a 400 ci engine.

Production

1977 Mark V	80,321
1978 Mark V	72,602
Diamond Jubilee	5,159
Cartier	8,520
Pucci	3,125
Givenchy	917
Blass	3,975
1979 Mark V	75,939

Market history

The Mark V remains a wonderful final statement of the big personal Lincolns. The conclusion of the production in that somber spring of fuel-short 1979 was a blessing in disguise. The Mark Vs were not hit so hard as earlier big cars because with only three years of production, values were still high. Inflation also helped to hold prices steady.

This 1977 Givenchy edition was in dark jade metallic paint with chamois color vinyl roof front panel. Designer Series have slightly more collector appeal. *Ford Motor Company*

The Bill Blass edition had this carriage roof, a faux cabriolet. This is the 1978 Mark V, and some collectors have been drawn to this distinctive look. The three-year production of the Mark V was very strong. *Lincoln-Mercury Division*

117

This is one of the 1979 Designer Series on the Mark V. This would be the last year of production and when the fuel crisis hit, the remaining stocks were sold with some difficulty. The three different years of the Mark V are visually very much alike and if there are doubts, check the VIN plate. *Ford Motor Company*

Thus Mark V used values never sank to the lower levels of the Mark IV or the Lincoln Continentals of the seventies.

At the end of 1981, the 1977 Mark V was bringing perhaps $7,000, according to the Kelley Blue Book. Three years later it was $5,500. From the standpoint of conventional used car marketing, the Mark V has continued to lose value but very slowly, so that in the late eighties, average values were in the $3,000 to $4,000 range. Designers Series and Diamond Jubilee cars were bringing a premium.

But there is evidence that in the nineties the Mark V will depart from normal market trends. Even as early as 1988, auction prices were beginning to show some "spikey" highs, breaking into five figures with a rare sale at $15,000 to $17,000. These auction prices compared favorably with Mark IV prices and were clearly higher than Mark III prices. Buyers are thus not conventional collectors of historic vehicles in which vehicle age usually means increased value. The buyers of the Mark V seem to be seeking the big Lincoln image. If the Mark III, IV and V are seen as parallel images of the big personal car, then why not buy the last production which will have the maximum number of features and refinement and will likely have the least wear?

Thus, the nineties may show the Mark V as having remarkable price gains. Ample supply of well-conditioned cars will make appreciation slow, but the fine low mileage cars may well move up into startling prices.

Chapter 14

1977–80 Lincoln Versailles

History

The new small Lincoln Versailles was announced on January 20, 1977. It was based on the successful Mercury Monarch, which had a 109.9–inch chassis and a 351 ci engine. For California, a 302 ci was specified. The handsome Mark V type radiator grille was fitted. The Versailles was trimmed to the same high standards as the Lincoln Continental, and most of the power options and deluxe features were available. The penalty of features was weight and the Versailles weighed 3,916 pounds compared to 3,404 pounds for the Monarch. The axle ratio was raised to 2.75:1 from 2.47:1 to restore performance.

Lincoln planners had an eye on the Cadillac Seville which had been launched in May 1975 and had supplied most of Cadillac's volume growth since that time. A response to the growing popularity of the compact luxury car as expressed in Mercedes and Jaguar was also a reason. Furthermore, the gasoline crunch in 1974 had shaken confi-

The 1977 Versailles was based on the Mercury Monarch and was Lincoln's answer to the Cadillac Seville. It was priced directly against the Continental Mark V which was not understood by the traditional Lincoln buyer, yet 15,434 were sold in the first year. Ardeth Conkle owns this fine example. *L.C.O.C.*

The frontal appearance of the 1977 Versailles followed the Mark V influence, as did the whole Lincoln line. *L.C.O.C.*

The 1978 Versailles was virtually unchanged from the 1977 model. Production fell sharply as buyers saw the car as an uptrimmed Mercury Monarch; but gasoline shortages in the eighties helped to hold up the value of these cars. *Ford Motor Company*

dence in the very big car, and management was going to respond to the GM downsizing challenge.

The Versailles was priced directly against the Mark V and well above the Continental, a bold move which followed Seville price strategy. Traditional Lincoln buyers, accustomed to the sales pitch of "bigger and better," were clearly not about to opt for a smaller sedan at a higher price. There were a small number of buyers interested in compact luxury and 15,434 of them lined up for the opening year of Versailles production.

The 1978 Versailles standardized the 302 engine, now giving 139 bhp while the lower compression California model gave only 133 bhp. There were very few changes. Sales were very slow and production totaled only 8,931 for the year.

A revision of the greenhouse occurred for 1979 in an effort to distance the Versailles from the Monarch. The rear section was extended and squared off and given the Town Car treatment complete with a coach-lamp. Luxury was everywhere, and the inte-

The roof of the 1979 Versailles was extended eight inches and given a new more vertical window. The Town Car roof padding helped to set the car apart. Sales picked up at once to a record for the series at 21,007 sold. *Ford Motor Company*

The final version of the Versailles was a poor seller because the new 1980 downsized Lincoln Continental was aimed at the same market. Collectors have been lukewarm to the Versailles for it had neither size nor power. But trim quality was as high as anything in the Lincoln lineup and the car had features beyond the competition. As the cars age and the supply diminishes, the Versailles may yet prove to be a sought after speciality car. *Ford Motor Company*

rior trim work was as good as anything in the Lincoln line. Sales improved.

The Versailles was left virtually untouched for 1980. Production ended in the summer.

Serial numbers

The first digit indicates the year: 1977 = 7, and so on.

The letter H = 351 ci engine in 1977.

The letter F = 302 ci engine used in 1977 for California and standard for all thereafter.

The code number for the Versailles is 84.

For example, 7(–)84 (H)80001 is a 1977 Versailles with a 351 ci engine.

Production
1977—15,434
1978—8,931
1979—21,007
1980—4,784

Problem areas

On rare occasions, the Versailles may stop on the road; if such a failure is instantaneous, check the EEC (Electronic Engine Control) unit on the left fender. A sharp rap may bring it back to life. The power steering hose may be too close to the exhaust manifold and could cause a fire.

Market history

The four brief years of the Versailles were Lincoln's first timid step into the compact luxury market. It was a holding action until the downsizing could take place in 1980, at which time the Versailles no longer filled a market target.

But in the used car market the car profited from the 1979 fuel crisis, and values held up very well in the early eighties. Somewhere in the mid-eighties the Versailles values reached somewhat of a parity with Continental prices. As the decade drew to a close, the 1977 and 1978 Versailles were selling ahead of the Continental. The 1979 model was selling for about the same price as the 1979 Continental.

Few Versailles appear at auction and the market is thin.

The future of the Versailles in the nineties is uncertain. It is a relatively low production car with a different image, which should help appreciation. The 1979 and 1980 models with the Town Car treatment are even more distinctive, though some fanciers prefer the earlier style.

Is the Versailles collectible? The normal Lincoln collector is drawn by size and power; the Versailles has neither. Yet the discernment which drew original buyers, namely a truly medium-sized car built to ultimate luxury standards, may yet draw collectors. The Versailles offers marvelous features not found in the Seville, Mercedes and Jaguar. As a very drivable speciality car, the Versailles remains a fine choice.

Chapter 15

★ | **All**

1980–83 Continental Mark VI

History

The Continental Mark VI was designed and marketed as a luxury version of the Lincoln Continental.

The 1980 Lincoln line was downsized and reorganized. For the first time the Mark nameplate included a four-door sedan, which was mounted on a 117.4–inch wheelbase. The Mark VI two door was on a 114.4–inch wheelbase. The Designer series continued on the two-door model and a new Signature series was optional on both the two door and the four door. The new Mark VI two door

picked up the styling themes of 1979 and managed to compress the themes successfully on the 114.4–inch wheelbase. The designer colors shifted again: Blass was in blue, Pucci in fawn, Givenchy in fawn and bittersweet (a copper tone), and Cartier in pewter.

Fuel economy was the key idea in 1980 and Lincoln attacked with substantial weight reduction. The Mark VI was down 775 pounds to 4,004 pounds. The Continental four door lost 800 pounds. The 302 ci engine was standard and had electronic fuel injec-

The new 1980 Mark VI now appeared in four-door form for the first time, which would continue throughout this series. The four door was on a 117.4 inch wheelbase, shared by the new Town Car and the Continental four door and two door. The two door Mark VI was alone on the 114.4 inch wheelbase. The Mark series

represented the top of the Lincoln line in what was a somewhat blurred product definition. This is a Signature series edition in metallic dark red and silver, substantially more expensive than the Designer coupe or the normal versions. Collectors will always go for the most deluxe version. *Ford Motor Company*

The two-door version of the Mark VI, in which much of the Mark V line was preserved. Weight was down almost 800 lbs., so even with the 302 ci engine, performance was still good. *Ford Motor Company*

The 1981 two door was little changed from 1980. The contrasting roof color adds interest; the wire wheels also help. Bob Kellner owns this car. *L.C.O.C.*

tion. Engine modifications included an electronic ignition control which affected all elements of the emissions system including fuel-air ratio, ignition timing, secondary air to exhaust emission system, exhaust gas recirculation flow and the purging of the evaporative emission canister. Sensors provided input; the black box had arrived. For 1980, only, there was an optional 351 ci V-8 with a variable-venturi carburetor. Economy was also helped by a four-speed automatic transmission with a lockup in the fourth gear. The battery size was reduced and a mini-spare was used.

Electronics were everywhere. Twelve buttons on the instrument panel computed numerous functions including speed in miles or kilometers, distance to empty tank, various clock functions and a trip log. This monitor also checked brake pressure, alternator, oil pressure, engine temperature, low washer level, trunk ajar, door ajar and various lamp outages. Warnings would automatically appear on the readout.

Sales of the new car began amid bulging inventory caused by the Iranian fuel shortage. The supply of Mark Vs on August 1, 1979, was 210 days. This inventory had shrunk to 135 days by November 1, but many dealers had Mark Vs available in 1980. Mark VI sales for the 1980 model year were only 38,891.

The Mark VI four door on the 117.4-inch wheelbase and the two-door version on the 114.4-inch wheelbase would continue through 1983.

The Mark VI had remarkable styling stability through the four years of production. In 1981 the Designer series was priced below the Signature series but this was reversed in 1982. For 1982, the four door was styled by Pucci. The two door continued Bill Blass and Givenchy treatments. In 1983 the Blass two door and Pucci four door were continued. There were few other minor changes. The 302 ci engine continued and now produced 134 bhp. It used the same block as the highly tuned Boss 302, which had produced 290 bhp in 1969. Smog emission controls had choked this great engine to a shadow of its old strength.

Serial numbers

The year of manufacture is readily verified from the Vehicle Identification Number, which changes radically after 1981. Up to and including 1980, the year of manufacture is the first digit. (0 = 1980). Beginning in 1981, an alphabetical system was used (B = 1981, C = 1982, D = 1983, E = 1984, F = 1985, G = 1986, H = 1987, J = 1988, K = 1989, L = 1990). The 302 ci engine used throughout the series is indicated by the letter F. Do not confuse this letter with the 1985 year code F at the end of the VIN. The letter P followed by two digits indicates the body type but the numbers are not used consistently throughout production.

Some examples are:

0 (-) 89 F 600001 = a 1980 2-dr Mark VI

1LM (-) P95FXB (-) 600001 = a 1981 2-dr Mark VI

1MRBP96F0C (-) 000001 = a 1982 4-dr Mark VI

1MRBP98FXD (-) 000001 = a 1983 2-dr Mark VI

Production

Year	Body	Number
1980	2-dr	20,647
	4-dr	18,244
	Total	38,891
1981	2-dr	18,740
	4-dr	17,958
	Total	36,698
1982	2-dr	11,532
	4-dr	14,804
	Total	26,336
1983	2-dr	12,743
	4-dr	18,113
	Total	30,856

The two-door version of the Mark VI was held to tight dimensions on the smaller wheelbase. This 1982 Bill Blass edition with the carriage roof shows continuity from the Mark V. In 1980 and 1981 the two door outsold the four door as Mark VI buyers continued to see the coupe as the traditional expression of the heritage. The Mark VI may now be quietly moving into collector status. This example is owned by Robert Kellner. L.C.O.C.

The 1981 Mark VI four door continues the rear quarter panel port hole, an identifying feature. Though this car was the "standard" model, trim and finish was superb. The Designer and Signature series may bring more money which could mean bargains for fine clean examples. *Ford Motor Company*

Market history

The following are the factory list prices of the base two-door Mark VI:

1980—$16,049
1981—$17,539
1982—$19,958
1983—$20,939

At the top of the Mark VI line was the Signature series four door:

1980—$21,902
1981—$23,519
1982—$23,226
1983—$24,321

The Designer series prices were originally lower than the Signature series but in 1982 were priced higher.

In the tumultuous market of the early eighties, the big cars struggled. By the summer of 1985, the five-year-old 1980 Mark VI was selling for about 50 percent of the new price. This rate of fall averaged approximately $1,700 per year. It would have been worse had not the rapid escalation of the new car prices helped to hold up the used market.

As new prices continued to rise, the Mark VI market stabilized and average retail prices for the same 1980 car fell by the summer of 1989 from around $8,000 to $6,000, only about $500 per year. One wonders whether or not these Mark VI Lincolns may be gradually moving into collector

This 1982 Designer two door has the Givenchy treatment; the Designer series was now again at the top of the line. Trim was lavish. *Ford Motor Company*

The 1982 Pucci four door appears to be at the top of the used market for Mark VIs of this year. The four-door Mark VIs in the normal used car market have brought more money than the two-door version. Whether this will apply to a future collectors market remains to be seen. *Ford Motor Company*

The 1983 Bill Blass two-door Mark VI was the most recognizable of the Designer series. It was also the most expensive Lincoln with a factory base price of $25,242. The most attractive Mark VIs may be bottoming out in value, a sign that collecting is about to begin. *Ford Motor Company*

The Designer Series Bill Blass edition was always a standout with the carriage roof, a faux convertible. The 1980 Mark VI adapts particularly well to this treatment. When collectibility begins, collectors will seek out the "different," and the Blass edition may catch their fancy. *Ford Motor Company*

status. The arrival of the new rounded Mark VII highlighted the square styling of the Mark VI which was more in the traditional Mark mode.

It may well be that the Mark VI prices of the early years have now reached bottom at around $6,000. Keep in mind that a beautiful clean 1983 Designer series Mark VI in the summer of 1989 could still approach five figures. Buyers of the Mark VI cars should keep a close look on market trends. There may be some signals from the auction trade, namely strongly priced true sales in which Mark VIs begin to appreciate. This will, at the very least, mean that the regular market depreciation is ended. That such recent Lincoln production can have price-appreciation possibilities in the nineties is a tribute to the success of the marque in the eighties.

1980 and 1982-87 Lincoln Continental

History

The Lincoln Continental line-up was re-defined between 1980 and 1982 and the various nameplates were shifted.

The new Lincoln Continental for 1980 was built on a 117.4–inch wheelbase which would be a standard Lincoln platform in the eighties. The new Mark VI four door would be on the same chassis and appeared as a deluxe version of the Continental. However, the Continental was offered in a two-door version on a 117.4–inch chassis while the Mark VI two door was on a 114.4–inch chassis.

The overall length of the Continental was reduced by 13.8 inches and weight dropped dramatically, the four door from 4,843 pounds to 4,038 pounds. The styling of the new car was very angular and boxy which preserved interior space. Interior dimensions were up from 1979, a remarkable achievement.

The special version of the Continental was called the Town Car which added coach lamps on the B-pillar, twin comfort lounge seats and other amenities.

The downsized Continental used the 302 ci engine, a member of the "90 degree V–8

The 1980 Lincoln Continental Town Car was built on the 117.4 inch wheelbase and was priced about $1,600 below the Mark VI. There was much similarity between the two four-door models. Prices for the Continental continue to be lower than for the Mark VI. *Ford Motor Company*

series." This venerable design began in 1962 as a 221 ci block and was used in the Fairlane and Mercury Meteor. In 1963 it was enlarged to the 260 ci and in 1964 to the famous 289 ci block. In 1968 it was again enlarged to 302 ci. The same tooling was used in the production of the "Y block series" which was the original OHV V-8 Ford engine in 1954. The bore spacing is the same in the two series and, for example, a crank shaft from the 292 Y block will fit directly into a 302. Racers would sometimes use the steel 292 truck crank in the "90 degree V-8 series" engines for durability.

Thus the 302 was a long-proven engine of very great stamina and was a fine choice for the V-8 Lincolns of the eighties. The high horsepower ratings of the sixties were long gone and the engines were detuned which further added to long life. Brake horsepower was 129 on an 8.4:1 compression ratio. The 351W engine at 140 bhp was a 49-state option.

The 1980 Continental coupe is rare in that it was built on the long wheelbase chassis and for only one year. Only 7,177 were built; whether this rarity will eventually bring collector interest remains to be seen. A two door version of the Town Car was built only in 1982. *Lincoln-Mercury Division*

The Continental was reborn in 1982 with a totally new body mounted on the short 108.8-inch wheelbase. The styling was "knife edge" in the manner of some British coachbuilders of the forties and fifties. Normal used car depreciation continues on this car and collecting possibilities will only begin when bottom price stability occurs. On average this occurs about fifteen years after a model is introduced. *Ford Motor Company*

Sales were down drastically in 1980 for the industry and in 1981 the Continental was discontinued.

The Continental returned in 1982 as a brand new car, downsized again on a 108.6-inch wheelbase. It was more than simply a smaller Versailles, though it was aiming at the same compact luxury market. The styling was novel, with razor edge surfaces reminiscent of the British coachbuilders H. J. Mulliner and Freestone and Webb. The belt line had a pleasing arch from front to rear which relieved the razor edging and produced a novel harmony. The Signature and Givenchy Designer series were introduced as deluxe trim and color levels.

The 302 engine was now standard across the Lincoln line. A new optional V–6 engine appeared with a 232 ci displacement but lasted only a year as few opted for its even lower 112 bhp. It would reappear in the 1988 revised Continental, with 140 bhp.

The reception for the new car was not bad with 23,908 sales. Lincoln management had hoped for 40,000 units but the opening year would turn out to be very close to the average annual sale of 22,678 for this model during the six-year run.

For 1983, the Signature series was dropped and the Valentino Designer series was added. The 302 engine was rated at 134 bhp. Trim was upgraded but sales declined.

In 1984, the grille was tilted and the aerodynamics were improved. The Givenchy series used blue colors and the Valentino series was in Cabernet wine colors. The 302 engine was now producing 140 bhp. The optional 302 with dual exhaust produced 155 bhp. Another option was a BMW turbo diesel of 149 ci displacement and 115 bhp. It was a better engine than the ill-fated GM Cadillac unit, but the diesel vogue was passing and the option was dropped in mid–1985. Sales nearly doubled in 1984 and it would be the best year for the six-year model.

In 1985, the splendid four-wheel anti-lock braking system was introduced as an option. The Givenchy series was now dark rosewood with mulberry brown interiors. Options abounded such as the keyless entry system, power deck lid pull down and a mobile phone.

For 1986, the 302 ci engine's compression was raised from 8.4:1 to 8.9:1, raising horsepower to 150. Torque moved up to 270 lb-ft. The anti-lock brake system was standard

This is the Givenchy edition of the 1983 Continental in black and platinum mist. The Valentino edition was painted walnut moondust and golden mist. The 302 ci engine was used across the Lincoln line and was rated at 134 bhp. *Ford Motor Company*

The grille was tilted back on the 1984 models and a sales record resulted for the series of 30,468. For the next three years there were only modest changes in the Continental. *Ford Motor Company*

The 1988 Continental was introduced in 1987. It was a total departure from the previous design and echoed the Taurus and Mark VII rounded look. The 232 ci V-6 engine was reintroduced following a brief use in 1982. A new model of such radical change helps enthusiasts to reappraise the previous styling ideas, a preliminary step toward collectibility. *Ford Motor Company*

across the line. Many interior treats awaited the buyer including power seat recliners, compass and thermometer, dual illuminated vanity mirrors, four-way headrests, keyless entry and a leather-wrapped steering wheel. The Givenchy treatment was in black and red velvet paint.

1987, the final year of the angular Continental, saw few changes. The Givenchy colors were rose quartz metallic over dark taupe metallic. The genuine walnut trim was replaced by a cherry wood applique. Production ended early in preparation for the new 1988 V–6–engined round-shaped Continental.

Serial numbers

The first digit is the year: 0 = 1980, 1 = 1981; thereafter the year is a letter at the end of the code just prior to the build number of the car (1982 = C, 1983 = D, 1984 = E, 1985 = F, 1986 = G, 1987 = H, 1988 = J).

The engine code F = 302 ci.

For examples, 0(–)82 F 600001 denotes a 1980 sedan with a 302 ci engine.

After 1982 the code is exceedingly complex and varies from year to year. For simple dating purposes the last letter only is important.

Production

1980	Continental	24,056
	Coupe	7,177
	Total	31,233
1981	Continental	no production
1982	Continental	
	(mid-size all new)	23,908
1983	Continental	16,831
1984	Continental	30,468

1985	Continental	28,253
1986	Continental	19,012
1987	Continental	17,597

Market history

The handsome 1982 Continental had a relatively short life. The similarity to the K Body Cadillac Seville was obvious but the Continental was more sharply sculptured and the surfaces were more tightly controlled. The short 108–inch wheelbase was a factor. The Continental had more power than the Seville and was closer to the target of a compact luxury car such as the Mercedes. However, on head-to-head competition, the Seville outsold the Continental.

Through the eighties, the Seville was priced one to two thousand dollars higher than the Continental. In the used market, the Continental fared very well with depreciation comparable or less than the Seville.

Will this Continental become a collectible? The normal used car strategies are still in place and will be through the nineties as the Continental depreciates to some eventual floor price. There are a lot of Continentals on the road and with values still very substantial for even the earliest 1982 models, junking will not occur in the near future.

The Continental is a handsome automobile, yet styled in an idiom which already seems dated. As a mid-sized four-door sedan, it may have only limited collector interest since it offers neither large size nor novelty. But the sharp angularity may yet find enthusiasts as the nineties decade proceeds. Again, the collector will keep an eye on the floor price and will have to measure the tradeoff of a long hold versus relatively slow future appreciation. (For comments on the 1980 Continental see the Town Car section.)

1981–89 Lincoln Town Car

History

The name "Continental" was deleted for the year 1981 and the "Town Car" became the only Lincoln offering. Thus began one of the most successful Ford products of the eighties. The squared body had been introduced in 1980 as the standard four door for both the Lincoln and Mark VI lines. The Town Car trim option for the Lincoln was popular in both two- and four-door forms and thus became the nameplate. The deluxe trimmed version was now called the Signature Series which included power outside mirrors, six-way adjustable right front seat, lighted armrest storage bins and identification scripts.

The 302 ci engine (code F) was continued and would be the standard V–8 engine for the eighties. Mechanical changes were minor.

The Town Car became an independent model in 1981, after being a trim option in 1980. It achieved unparalleled success during the decade. A comparison of the various year models demonstrates the virtually unchanged styling. Here is the original 1981 Town Car. *Ford Motor Company*

The Town Car nameplate was focused in 1982 with the dropping of the two-door body. Henceforth the Town Car comprised just one four-door design which would be unchanged through the decade, a brilliant marketing move. Lincoln planners had achieved the stability of image which Cadillac once enjoyed but was now rapidly losing through downsizing. The Signature Series was continued at a $3,000 premium. For an additional $1,020, the Cartier Designer Series was added at the top of the line using light pewter and opal color tones.

The 1983 Lincoln was refined but with no major changes. The Lincoln image and sales were helped by the new emphasis on quality. The "Lincoln Commitment" had been introduced in 1982 along with extended warranties. The public was being convinced that the Town Car was the quality large car. The Cartier Designer Series used charcoal moondust and platinum mist colors. Radios were

The 1983 Cartier edition was the top of the line. The little medallion on the front fender panel reads "electric fuel injection," useful in meeting emissions controls on the 302 ci engine. Sales were slowly climbing. *Ford Motor Company*

Sales climbed steeply in 1984 as Lincoln stayed with a proven formula. Collecting possibilities for the Town Car remain distant because of the very large production. *Ford Motor Company*

134

A grille change to small rectangular patterns identifies the 1985 Town Car. Sales set a record of 119,878. This car, like other Town Cars, might become collectible around the turn of the century if past experience is any indication. *Ford Motor Company*

upgraded, the day-night mirror was automatically dimmed, an anti-theft system was offered and the garage door opening systems was improved. The Town Car was becoming an entertainment.

The 1984 Town Car continued to refine an already sumptuous specification. A low oil warning light was a useful idea. The Cartier Designer Series stayed in the neutral colors with Arctic white and grays.

For 1985, some minor styling changes marked the next generation of this superb design, the most noticeable of which were the slightly angled taillights and a new grille pattern. The Signature and Cartier Designer Series continued. Front seats now reclined on all models, a rather tardy acceptance of longstanding European practice. The keyless entry system fascinated buyers. Another nice touch on the Cartier Series was a power trunk lid closing system.

In 1986, horsepower moved up to 150 on all models from the trusty 302 ci engine. The Cartier Designer Series continued to use gray color tones. The Signature Series of-

In 1987, the Town Car still was selling well after six years in production. *Ford Motor Company*

fered the carriage roof option, an all cloth convertible look. A J. B. Lansing sound system was available with twelve speakers.

Minor refinements marked the 1987 car. The mechanical success of the car prompted a further extension of the warranty to a 48–month, 50,000 mile for mechanical parts and a 60–month, 100,000 mile for corrosion. The Signature and the Designer Series continued. A special edition was the "Sail America" model which was connected with Ford's sponsorship of the America's Cup Challenge.

The 302 ci engine continued at 150 bhp for 1988; EPA fuel mileages were 17 city and 24 highway. The price of the base Town Car was now $25,591; the Signature, $27,898; and the Cartier edition, $29,044. The basic successful themes continued.

The year 1989 would see the last production of this extraordinarily stable design. Prices would continue to edge up—the base car now $26,806, the Signature $29,113 and the Cartier edition at $30,259. The Cartier edition was still cheaper than the lowest priced Mercedes, the 2.5 liter diesel, at $31,230. Many buyers would see the Town Car as a great bargain and sales continued briskly.

Production

1981	Town Car and Town coupe	32,839
	Coupe and Signature coupe	4,935
	Sedan	27,904

1982	Town Car	35,069
1983	Town Car	53,381
1984	Town Car	93,622
1985	Town Car	119,878
1986	Town Car	117,771
1987	Town Car	76,483
1988	Town Car	201,113
1989	Town Car	128,533

Market history

The Lincoln Town Car is the success story of the decade. From a modest beginning in 1980, a year of general disaster for the industry, the Town Car steadily went on from strength to strength, building to extraordinary volumes.

There are several reasons for this success. First and most importantly, the image of the car was stabilized and, through shrewd marketing, was able to convey to the buying public a new standard of full-size luxury. The body was unchanged throughout the decade. Refinements were steady. As is the case with all production, the car improved with age.

The 1988 Cartier edition of the Town Car. Sales reached an extraordinary 201,113 Town Cars— a record. With other Lincoln production, the Division beat Cadillac in absolute numbers for the first time. *Ford Motor Company*

Secondly, Town Car sales were helped by the stumbling of Cadillac which changed image in the middle of the decade. The 1985 Deville and Fleetwood were shrunk from a 121.5-inch wheelbase to 110.8 inches and the overall length dropped from 221 to 195 inches. The following year, the Seville and Eldorado were downsized. The wheelbase went from 114 to 108 inches and overall length dropped from 204 to 188 inches. These were very great changes and the public reacted strongly. In 1986, Seville sales fell one half and the Eldorado sales fell 72 percent. Traditional Cadillac buyers began to look at the Town Car as the last remaining domestic luxury automobile.

A third factor helped the Town Car. Cadillac engine innovation in the early eighties was not successful. The 8-6-4 V-8 unit designed for economy turned out to be unreliable and was withdrawn quickly but not before bad publicity sullied the marque. Even more disastrous was the diesel program. Substantial numbers of the engines in the field failed and dragged down the Cadillac market. Meanwhile, the Town Car used the old reliable 302 ci engine. Horsepower was gradually increased as engineers found ways of meeting emissions controls. The Town Car had a well-deserved reputation of reliability.

Thus as the eighties unfolded, the Town Car volume increased, culminating in a 1988 production of 201,113 units. This, coupled with the Continental and Mark VII production, produced a grand total of 280,659 cars, an all-time record which also handily beat Cadillac's total production of 270,844, another first.

A fourth factor entered into the market, namely rising prices. The following chart shows the Town Car sedan's lowest base price:

1981—$14,958
1982—$16,880
1983—$17,916
1984—$19,069
1985—$19,756
1986—$21,473
1987—$23,361
1988—$25,591
1989—$26,806

The Signature Series sold about $3,000 above the sedan base price and the Designer Series about $5,000 above the base sedan price. Thus Lincoln prices at the beginning of the decade were under $20,000 and at the end of the decade were well over $30,000.

This increase had a tonic effect on the used car market, tending to limit depreciation. The Town Car retained value very well

The final year for the old-style Town Car was 1989 and this Signature edition is remarkably similar to the 1981 model. Such stability in design is a great tribute to Lincoln stylists. *Ford Motor Company*

137

The Town Car was completely redesigned for 1990 and is shown here in the Cartier Designer Series. Variable assist power steering, rear load leveling and two front seat air-bags were new features. Initial sales were subsequently above the 1989 model. One wonders if this handsome fresh design will be able to equal the decade long success of the prior model. *Lincoln-Mercury Division*

through the decade. It was the best performer of the Lincoln products and also ranked above some of the Cadillac models.

In the light of this popularity, the question is whether or not the Town Car will become a collectible. The signal for collecting will be that point at which the used market resists further decline. Now that the original design has been superseded, the pool of cars will begin to shrink. But there are a lot of Town Cars out there and they are cared for by loving owners. If past performance is any guide, a floor should be reached about five years after the last model is produced. Thus, in the mid-nineties, the Town Car market should be carefully watched. A reappearance of a fuel shortage or further downsizing of cars to meet economy requirements may speed the collectibility of these cars even at the time when panic selling could take place.

Meanwhile, the pleasure from driving these lavishly equipped cars remains and owners can drive with the hope of a future potential.

★★	Luxury Sports Coupe
★	All others

1984–90 Continental Mark VII

History

The new Continental Mark VII was previewed in June 1983 in three variations, a standard base car, the LSC (Luxury Sports Coupe) performance model and the Designer Series. The LSC had high-performance steering and tires, black wall tires, digital instruments, leather-wrapped wheel but no tachometer. Flush-fitting halogen lamps were a US industry first.

The 302 ci engine produced 140 bhp and was mated to a four-speed automatic transmission with a locking torque converter. A 2.4 liter six-cylinder Turbo-charged diesel was available with 115 bhp. Four-wheel disc brakes were standard. Technical novelty was in the electronic air suspension, four rubber canisters with a compressor, sensors and a microcomputer to alter suspension to fit road needs. Automatic static leveling was a bonus.

Tim Howley, editor of *Continental Comments*, sagely observed that the car is more reminiscent of the Thunderbird than the Mark VI. The wheelbase was 108.6 inches, down thirteen inches from the Mark VI. Weight was 3,625 pounds, 350 pounds lighter than the Mark VI and thirteen inches shorter. The Mark VII was much more a driver's car and a bold new step for the Ford Motor Company.

The Designer Series featured a Bill Blass edition using goldenrod mist over harvester wheat mist paint with complementary interior colors. The Gianni Versace treatment was painted walnut moondust, with desert tan interior.

Some bells and whistles included a compass, ice alert digital instrument, power deck lid closer, CB radio, front seat heaters, garage door opener, security system and a moonroof. A handling package was available for the Designer Series.

The Mark VII was well received but criticism was heard of the low power-to-weight ratio. A high-performance version of the

The Mark series had been evolutionary until the Mark VII, which was a very sharp break from previous styling ideas. Not only was the styling in the new rounded idiom but a performance oriented edition appeared in the Luxury Sport Coupe (LSC). The Designer Series included Bill Blass and Gianni Versace. Shown is the 1984 Mark VII previewed in June, 1983. *Ford Motor Company*

302 engine was offered for 1985 with 180 bhp and 260 lb-ft of torque. The standard 302 engine continued to produce 140 bhp; the diesel option also continued, but with few takers. The anti-lock brake system was standard across the line. The Bill Blass edition used silver sand metallic over burnished pewter metallic and the Gianni Versace used a navy metallic exterior with admiral blue interiors. Total Mark VII sales were low.

For 1986, the optional high-performance engine was raised to 200 bhp with 285 lb-ft of torque. Compression was 9.2:1. The standard engine compression was raised from 8.4:1 to 8.9:1, raising power up to 150. The Mark VII was now known as the Lincoln Mark VII, and to emphasize the point, the word "Lincoln" replaced "Continental" on body lettering. The Bill Blass edition continued with sandalwood tones.

Minor changes marked 1987 Mark VII specifications. The Town Car rear axle ratio of 3.08:1 was available to take advantage of higher power and to improve economy. The Bill Blass colors were prairie mist metallic in two tones.

The 1985 LSC featured a new tuned version of the 302 ci engine producing 180 bhp. The public was still finding the Mark VII and sales were down. *Ford Motor Company*

The 1987 LSC continued the 200 bhp engine introduced in 1986. Sales totals were artificially low because of the early introduction of the 1988 models. As a personal touring car, the LSC was finding many friends. *Ford Motor Company*

For 1988, the power was again increased. The 302 engine boasted 225 bhp and 300 lb-ft of torque. The Bill Blass Edition had the 3.03:1 axle while the LSC used the 3.27:1 ratio. The alternator capacity had been steadily moving upward and was now 100 amperes. The LSC series offered optional leather sports seats with lateral support while the Blass edition offered both cloth and leather luxury seats. Electronic instruments were standard on the Blass edition. The LSC used analog gauges. Traction-lok differentials were available.

There were virtually no changes for the 1989 model year. For 1990 a new instrument panel was introduced plus a driver's side air bag. The LSC model had new cast aluminum wheels.

Production
1984—33,344
1985—18,355
1986—20,056
1987 (short year production)—15,286
1988 (begin Feb. 1987)—38,259
1989—29,658
Total—154,958

Market history
The Mark VII was a sensational new idea in 1983 and received strong notices from reviewers. The new rounded lines were typical of the trend-setting new Ford cars. The Mark VII had a purposeful look and was perceived as more of driving car than the Mark VI. The LSC series catered to this image with analog gauges and seating with improved lateral support.

Sales were up and down in the eighties, in part a reflection of Cadillac's successes and failures. The Mark VII was able to maintain a consistent image, and once traditional Lincoln buyers became accustomed to the new size and shape, support grew.

The principle competition for the Mark VII was the Cadillac Eldorado. Mark VII depreciation was consistently lower than the Eldorado as the public reacted favorably to Lincoln products. In particular, the 1986 downsized Eldorado on the 108–inch wheelbase failed to find market support. In 1989 a three-year-old Eldorado could command only 58 percent of its new price while the Mark VII was selling at 75 percent of first cost.

Whenever there is strong acceptance of a model, chances improve for future collectibility, especially in a two-door personal luxury car. The Mark VII may well be one of those cars. The car was steadily improved, power had risen and the company has been responsive to customer desires. The sheer

The 1989 LSC was little changed after five years, but refinements continued. Collectibility for these cars cannot be expected before the turn of the century. *Ford Motor Company*

luxury of these cars is beyond criticism, but the sporting version of the LSC may find particular interest.

Normal used car strategies will prevail as long as the Mark VII remains in production.

But here again, the Lincoln magic, so remarkable in the eighties, may enable the Mark VII to be one of those rare cars which can be enjoyed when new and can then subtly become a long-term investment.

The 1990 Continental offered minor styling revisions. The unified design of this model was well received and sales advanced for 1990. *Lincoln-Mercury Division*

The 1990 Mark VII, shown here in the LSC Series, offered new aluminum road wheels and seat modifications. As a compact personal road car, it continued to find a large number of buyers. In the long run, two door cars of this type will probably prove to be the most collectible. *Lincoln-Mercury Division*

Appendix

The Lincoln Continental Owner's Club was formed in 1953 and the first membership list was published in July 1953 with 153 members. The focus of the club was on the V-12-engined cars. By 1960 the club had grown to 625 members. In June 1965 the club had reached 900 members; one year later membership exceeded 1,100. Membership in 1990 was about 3,600.

The recognition of the classic potential of the Mark II was the impetus for a broadening of membership. The successes of the 1961 Continental and the Mark III, IV and V further expanded the club. The addition of owners of the earliest Lincolns from 1920-1922, the 1923 to 1930 Model L, and the 1931 to 1940 Model K, KA, and KB models would bring the club to its logical final definition.

Ownership of cars for each era is *approximately* as follows:
Pre-1940—7%
1940-1942—14%
1946-1948—15%
1949-1951—2%
1952-1957—4%
Mark II—7%
1958-1960—6%
1961-1965—16%
1966-1969—9%
Mark III—10%
Mark IV—3%
Mark V—3%
Mark VI—2%
Mark VII—1%
Versailles—.5%
Town Car—1%
Miscellaneous—.5%

The primary focus of the club remains with the original 1936-1948 V-12 cars with more than 29 percent of members owning these cars. The second strong focus is the 1961 to 1969 cars with 25 percent of the number. The Mark III has another strong emphasis. On a percentage basis of original production, the Mark II probably wins.

The club offers a fine quarterly magazine, *Continental Comments*. Technical advice, regional and national meets, and tours are offered by the club.

Potential buyers of any Lincoln should join the club, not only for the above reasons, but to have access to the classified ads of club members. The address for further information is: The Lincoln & Continental Owners Club, 712 1st Ave., Seaside, Oregon 97138.

Bibliography

The Cars of Lincoln Mercury by George H. Dammann and James K. Wagner, Crestline Publications, Sarasota, Florida, 1987. 592 pages. A large format picture book arranged by year with full captions. A fine narrative text introduces each year's models. The best single source for Lincoln information.

Fifty Years of Lincoln Mercury by George H. Dammann, Crestline Publications, Glen Ellen, Illinois, 1971. 320 pages. Earlier edition of above book. Out of print.

Lincoln and Continental, The Post War Years by Paul R. Woudenberg, Motorbooks International, Osceola, Wisconsin, 1980. 152 pages. A technical and commercial history beginning in 1937 through 1980, with emphasis on management strategy and product development. Out of print.

The Lincoln Motorcar, Sixty Years of Excellence by Thomas E. Bonsall, Bookman Publishing, Baltimore, Maryland, 1981. 320 pages. A year-by-year history with representative pictures. Prefaces on Leland, Henry Ford, competitive makes, and a reprint of a Lincoln brochure, *How the Lincoln is Made* (circa 1929).

The Lincoln Continental by OCee Ritch, Clymer Publications, Los Angeles, 1963 (reprinted). An early study of the Lincoln including a 61–page reprint of the 1947 Repair Manual for the H Series V–12 engine.